THE VOYAGES OF CHRISTOPHER COLUMBUS

CHRISTOPHER COLUMBUS

The Voyages of
Christopher Columbus

by

Washington Irving

Edited by
Robert Owen

LONDON
THE PILOT PRESS LIMITED
1949

First Published in 1949 *by*
THE PILOT PRESS LTD.
45 GREAT RUSSELL ST.
W.C.1

Made and Printed in Great Britain by
TILLOTSONS (BOLTON) LTD.
AT MEALHOUSE LANE, BOLTON

Contents

CONTENTS—*continued*

Fourth Voyage 1502

List of Illustrations

Introduction

The Life and Voyages of Christopher Columbus by Washington Irving was first published in 1828. At that time it was the most complete and accurate account available. Written in a style similar to other literary classics from his pen, which include *Bracebridge Hall*, *Rip Van Winkle*, and *The Conquest of Granada*, the book has for many years been unobtainable.

Irving made full use of his gift for descriptive writing when recounting this story. He had long felt that an account of the voyages of Columbus should be available in the English tongue. More especially since the famous collection of documents in Spanish, relevant to the voyages of Columbus, had been published in 1826 by Don Martin Fernandez de Navarrete.

During the years from 1828, however, many additional documents and papers have come to light, and numerous books compiled; some historians completely agreeing with Irving, others arguing that his facts were from inaccurate and unreliable sources.

Irving collated his account by research among the many libraries and private collections of books which were put at his disposal when he visited Madrid. In his Introduction to the first edition of *Columbus*, he writes ". . . In the execution of this work I have avoided indulging in mere speculation or general reflections, excepting such as rose naturally out of the subject, preferring to give minute and circumstantial narrative, omitting no particular that appeared characteristic of the persons, the events, or the times; and endeavouring to place every fact in such a point of view, that the reader might perceive its merits, and draw his own maxims and conclusions".

The present volume is concerned with the narration of the voyages of discovery to the New World, and the trials, troubles, joys and disappointments Columbus faced between 1492 and 1505. The "Life" and account of the years leading up to his leaving Spain have been omitted. The bibliography at the end of this book will assist those who wish to study his early life, and read other accounts of the voyages.

It has proved necessary to include certain footnotes, and any which appear have been added in the editing; original footnotes having been incorporated into the text.

Before we turn to the *Voyages of Christopher Columbus* it may, perhaps, be useful to recall the state of the world at that time.

It was a wonderful and exciting period, and probably the most interesting in history. Europe was beginning to feel the Renaissance—in fact the entire known world was re-awakening to a revival of learning, bringing as it did new conceptions of philosophy, religion, art and literature; and a firmer grasp on invention and discovery.

In England the Wars of the Roses were in full force. Germany also had internal strife and war, and the peoples of these two nations, together with the French appeared dissatisfied and troubled; they were not fully aware of the great changes taking place, for not until the early part of the sixteenth century was the Renaissance greeted in Northern Europe.

In Southern Europe, however, this was a prosperous era. Italy, renowned as she was at this time for her commercial undertakings, enjoyed a wave of prosperity, which did not subside until the latter part of the fifteenth century, when Portugal and Spain with their new empires took control and changed the face of Europe and the World.

During the reign of Prince Henry the Navigator, who died in 1460, Portugal made immense progress in navigation and exploration. She attracted many astronomers, great men of science and those with maritime knowledge, and had become in this field of adventurous and hazardous undertakings far ahead of the rest of the world.

Spain, watching with some envy the fortunes of the Portuguese and their increasing empire had, in 1492, after the

Conquest of Granada, when the last Moorish stronghold was occupied, agreed that Columbus should undertake a voyage of discovery—to establish a route to the East by sailing across the unknown Atlantic Ocean, and further their Empire and plans for colonisation.

However, the greatest power in the world at this time was the Church of Rome. The Renaissance and the revival of learning had become a means of increasing its membership; the voyages of discovery and exploration (so frequently and successfully being carried out) were a new source of income, for the Church had demanded that part of all profits of discoveries be paid to them. It will be observed later that the voyages of Columbus were controlled and partly directed by the Church of Rome.

* * *

This, briefly, was the period in which Christopher Columbus lived.

He was born in Genoa about the year 1451, and had two brothers—Bartholomew and Diego—both of whom were later to play an important part in his life.

Columbus first went to sea at the age of fourteen years, probably sailing in normal commercial journeys to and from the many islands in the Mediterranean.

During 1476 he left Italy and sailed to Portugal, a country which as we know, had made great headway in exploration. Columbus possessed the theory of a sea route to Asia by sailing to the west.

For three years he sailed with the Portuguese fleet, and during a return voyage from an expedition to Guinea, decided he would put the idea of this new route to Asia to the King. After waiting four years he was received at the court, but demanded such exorbitant rewards for undertaking the command of such an expedition that his ideas were rejected.

He left Portugal for Spain in 1485 and submitted his plans to King Ferdinand and Queen Isabella. A further seven years elapsed before his proposals were again discarded. Spain had just ended a war against the Moors and could not afford such fantastic demands.

A dejected, but determined man, he resolved to go to King Charles VIII in France, but before crossing the border was recalled. Queen Isabella had agreed and an agreement was drawn up which *embodied all that Columbus had asked.*

This agreement, or capitulation contained words to the following effect:

i That Columbus should have for himself, during his life, and to his heirs and successors for ever, the office of High Admiral in all the seas, lands and continents he might discover.

ii That he should be Viceroy and Governor-General over all the lands and continents he might discover, with the privilege of nominating three candidates for the Government of such territories, the Sovereign nominating one candidate.

iii That he should be entitled to one-tenth of all merchandise and products found within his Admiralty.

iv That he, or his lieutenant, should be the sole judge of troubles and disputes arising out of trade and traffic between his Admiralty and Spain.

v That he might then, and at all times, contribute one-eighth part of the expenses of expeditions to countries he hoped to discover, and that he should receive one-eighth part of any profits.

This was signed by Ferdinand and Isabella on the 17th of April, 1492, at Sante Fé, near Granada. On the 12th of May, 1492, Columbus set out to Palos where he was to prepare for the voyage.

By the beginning of August of that year three vessels were ready for sea. They were the *Santa Maria*, on which Columbus had hoisted his flag, a decked ship of 100 tons and manned by a crew of 52 men; the *Pinta*, commanded by Martin Alonzo Pinzon, a caravel of 50 tons with 18 men, and a second caravel of 40 tons, the *Niña*, with 18 men commanded by Vincente Yañez Pinzon.

A religious service was held on August 2nd in the church of St. George at Palos. It was a solemn and impressive moment: Christopher Columbus and 90 men were about to voyage into the unknown—the greatest voyage of discovery the world has known.

FIRST VOYAGE, 1492

CHAPTER I

DEPARTURE FROM SPAIN—EVENTS DURING THE FIRST VOYAGE—DISCOVERY OF THE NEW WORLD

IT was early in the morning of Friday, the 3rd of August, 1492, that Columbus set sail from the bar of Saltes, a small island formed by the rivers Odiel and Tinto, in front of Palos, steering for the Canary Islands, from whence he intended to strike due west. As a guide by which to sail, he had the conjectural map or chart sent him by Paolo Toscanelli, of Florence.

AUGUST

On the third day after setting sail, the *Pinta* made signal of distress, her rudder being broken and unhung. This was suspected to have been done through the contrivance of the owners, Gomez Rascon and Christoval Quintero, to disable the vessel and cause her to be left behind. Columbus was much disturbed at this occurrence. It gave him a foretaste of the difficulties to be expected from people partly enlisted on compulsion, and full of doubt and foreboding. Trivial obstacles might, in this early stage of the voyage, spread panic and mutiny through his crews, and induce them to renounce the prosecution of the enterprise.

Martin Alonzo Pinzon, who commanded the *Pinta*, secured the rudder with cords, but these fastenings soon gave way, and the caravel proving defective in other respects. Columbus remained three weeks cruising among the Canary Islands in search of another vessel to replace her. Not being able to find one, the *Pinta* was repaired and furnished with a new rudder. The lateen sails of the *Niña* were also altered into square sails, that she might work more steadily and securely. While making these repairs, and taking in wood and water, Columbus was informed that three Portuguese caravels had been seen hovering off the island of Ferro. Dreading some hostile stratagem on the part of the King of Portugal, in revenge for his having embarked in the service of Spain, he put to sea early on the morning of the 6th of September, but for three days a profound calm detained the vessels within a short distance of the land. This was a tantalizing delay, for Columbus trembled lest something should occur to defeat his expedition, and was impatient to find himself far upon the ocean, out of sight of either land or sail; which, in the pure atmosphere of these latitudes, may be seen at an immense distance.

SEPTEMBER

On Sunday, the 9th of September, at daybreak, he saw Ferro about nine leagues distant; he was in the very neighbourhood, therefore, where the Portuguese caravels had been seen. Fortunately a breeze sprang up with the sun, and in the course of the day the heights of Ferro gradually faded from the horizon.

On losing sight of land, the hearts of the crews failed them, for they seemed to have taken leave of the world. Behind them was everything dear to the heart of man—country, family, friends, life itself; before them everything was chaos, mystery, and peril. In the anxiety of the moment they despaired of ever again seeing their homes. Many of the rugged seamen shed tears, and some broke into loud lamentations. Columbus tried in every way to soothe their distress, describing the splendid countries to which he expected to conduct them, and promising them land, riches, and everything that could arouse their interests or inflame their imaginations; nor were these promises made for purposes of deception, for he certainly believed he should realise them all.

He now gave orders to the commanders of the other vessels, in case they should be separated by any accident, to continue directly westward; and that, after sailing seven hundred leagues, they should lay by from midnight until daylight, as at about that distance he confidently expected to find land. Foreseeing that the vague terrors already awakened among the seamen would increase with the space which intervened between them and their homes, he commenced a stratagem which he continued throughout the voyage. This was to keep two reckonings, one private, in which the true way of the ship was noted, and which he retained in secret for his own government; the other public, for general inspection, in which a number of leagues was daily subtracted from the sailing of the ships, so as to keep the crews in ignorance of the real distance they had advanced.

When about one hundred and fifty leagues west of Ferro they fell in with part of a mast of a large vessel, and the crews, tremblingly alive to every omen, looked with a rueful eye upon this fragment of a wreck, drifting ominously at the entrance of these unknown seas.

On the 13th of September, in the evening, Columbus, for the first time, noticed the variation of the needle, a phenomenon which had never before been mentioned. He at first made no mention of it, lest his people should be alarmed; but it soon attracted the attention of the pilots, and filled them with consternation. It seemed as if the very laws of Nature were changing as they advanced, and that they were entering another world, subject to unknown influences. They apprehended that the compass was about to lose its mysterious virtues, and, without this guide, what was to become of them in a vast and trackless ocean? Columbus tasked his science and ingenuity for reasons with which to allay their terrors. He told them that the direction of the needle was not to the polar star, but to some fixed and invisible point. The variation, therefore, was not caused by any fallacy in the compass, but by the movement of the north star itself, which, like the other heavenly bodies, had its changes and revolutions, and every day described a circle round the pole. The high opinion they entertained of Columbus as a profound astronomer gave weight to his theory, and their alarm subsided.

They had now arrived within the influence of the trade wind, which, following the sun, blows steadily from east to west between the tropics, and sweeps over a few adjoining degrees of the ocean. With this propitious breeze directly aft, they were wafted gently but speedily over a tranquil sea, so that for many days they did not shift a sail. Columbus in his *Journal*[1] perpetually recurs to the bland and temperate serenity of the weather, and compares the pure and balmy mornings to those of April in Andalusia, observing that the song of the nightingale was alone wanting to complete the illusion.

They now began to see large patches of herbs and weeds, all drifting from the west. Some were such as grow about rocks or in rivers, and as green as if recently washed from the land. On one of the patches was a live crab. They saw also a white tropical bird, and tunny fish played about the ships. Columbus now supposed himself arrived in the weedy sea described by Aristotle, into which certain ships of Cadiz had been driven by an impetuous east wind.

As he advanced, there were various other signs that gave great animation to the crews; many birds were seen flying from the west; there was a cloudiness in the north, such as often hangs over land; and at sunset the imagination of the seamen, aided by their desires, would shape those clouds into distant islands. Every one was eager to be the first to behold and announce the wished-for shore; for the sovereigns had promised a pension of thirty crowns to whomsoever should first discover land.

Columbus sounded occasionally with a line of two hundred fathoms, but found no bottom. Martin Alonzo Pinzon, as well as others of his officers and many of the seamen, were often eager for Columbus to alter his course and steer in the direction of these favourable signs; but he persevered in steering to the westward, trusting that, by keeping in one steady direction, he should reach the coast of India, even if he should miss the intervening islands, and might then seek them on his return.

Notwithstanding the precaution which had been taken to keep the people ignorant of the distance they had sailed, they gradually became uneasy at the length of the voyage. The various indications of land which occasionally flattened their

[1] The *Journal* only referred to the First Voyage.

hopes passed away one after another, and the same interminable expanse of sea and sky continued to extend before them.

They had advanced much farther west than ever man had sailed before, and though already beyond the reach of succour, were still pressing onward and onward into that apparently boundless abyss. Even the favourable wind, which seemed as if providentially sent to waft them to the New World with such gentle breezes, was conjured by their fears into a source of alarm. They feared that the wind in these seas always prevailed from the east, and if so, would never permit their return to Spain.

A few light and gentle breezes from the west allayed, for a time, their apprehension; and several small birds, such as keep about groves and orchards, came singing in the morning, and flew away at night. Their song was wonderfully cheering to the hearts of the poor mariners, who hailed it as the voice of land. The birds they had hitherto seen had been large and strong of wing, but such small birds, they observed, were too feeble to fly far, and their singing showed that they were not exhausted by their flight.

On the following day there was a profound calm, and the sea, as far as the eye could reach, was covered with weeds, so as to have the appearance of a vast inundated meadow—a phenomenon attributed to the immense quantities of submarine plants which are detached by the currents from the bottom of the ocean. The seamen now feared that the sea was growing shallow; they dreaded lurking rocks and shoals and quicksands; and that their vessels might run aground, as it were, in the midst of the ocean, far out of the track of human aid, and with no shore where the crews could take refuge. Columbus proved the fallacy of this alarm by sounding with a deepsea line and finding no bottom.

For three days there was a continuance of light summer airs, from the southward and westward, and the sea was as smooth as a mirror. The crews now became uneasy at the calmness of the weather. They observed that the contrary winds they experienced were transient and unsteady, and so light as not to ruffle the surface of the sea; the only winds of constancy and force were from the west, and even they had not power to disturb the stillness of the ocean. There was a risk, therefore, either of perishing amidst stagnant and shoreless waters, or of being prevented by contrary winds from ever returning to their native country.

Columbus continued, with admirable patience, to reason with these absurd fancies, but in vain; when, fortunately, there came on a heavy swell of the sea, unaccompanied by wind—a phenomenon that often occurs in the broad ocean, caused by the impulse of some past gale or distant current of wind. It was, nevertheless, regarded with astonishment by the mariners, and dispelled the imaginary terrors occasioned by the calm.

The situation of Columbus was daily becoming more and more critical. The impatience of the seamen arose to absolute mutiny. They gathered together in the retired parts of the ships, at first in little knots of two and three, which gradually increased and became formidable, joining in murmurs and menaces against the Admiral. They exclaimed against him as an ambitious desperado who in a mad fantasy had determined to do something extravagant to render himself notorious. What obligation bound them to carry on with this voyage, or when were the terms of their agreement to be considered as fulfilled? They had already penetrated into seas untraversed by a sail, and where man had never before adventured. Were they to sail on until they perished, or until all return with their frail ships became impossible? Who would blame them should they consult their safety and return? The Admiral was a foreigner, a man without friends or influence. His scheme had been condemned by the learned as idle and visionary, and disapproved by people of all ranks. There was, therefore, no party on his side, but rather a large number who would be gratified by his failure.

Such are some of the reasonings by which these men prepared themselves for open rebellion. Some even proposed, as an effectual mode of silencing all after complaints of the Admiral, that they should throw him into the sea, and give out that he had fallen overboard while contemplating the stars and signs of the heavens, with his astronomical instruments.

Columbus was not ignorant of these secret intrigues, but he kept a serene and steady countenance, soothing some with gentle words, stimulating the pride or the avarice of others, and openly menacing the most refractory with punishment.

Hopes diverted them for a time. On the 25th of September Martin Alonzo Pinzon mounted on the stern of his vessel and shouted, "Land! land! Señor, I claim the reward!" There was, indeed, such an appearance of land in the southwest that Columbus threw himself upon his knees and returned thanks to God, and all the crews joined in chanting *Gloria in Excelsis.* The ships altered their course and stood all night to the southwest, but the morning light put an end to all their hopes as to a dream; the fancied land proved to be nothing but an evening cloud, and had vanished in the night.

For several days they continued on, with alternate hopes and murmurs, until the various signs of land became so numerous that the seamen, from a state of despondency, passed to one of high excitement. Eager to obtain the promised pension, they were continually giving the cry of land, until Columbus declared that should any one give a notice of the kind and land not be discovered within three days afterwards, he should forfeit all claim to the reward.

On the 7th of October they had come seven hundred and fifty leagues, the distance at which Columbus had computed to find the island of Cipango [Japan]. There were great flights of small field birds to the southwest, which seemed to indicate some neighbouring land in that direction, where they were sure of food and a resting-place. Yielding to the solicitations of Martin Alonzo Pinzon, Columbus, during the evening altered his course, therefore, to the west-southwest.

OCTOBER

Signs of land increased; birds came singing about the ships; and herbage floated by as fresh and green as if recently from shore. When, however, on the evening of the third day of this new course, the seamen saw the sun go down upon a shoreless

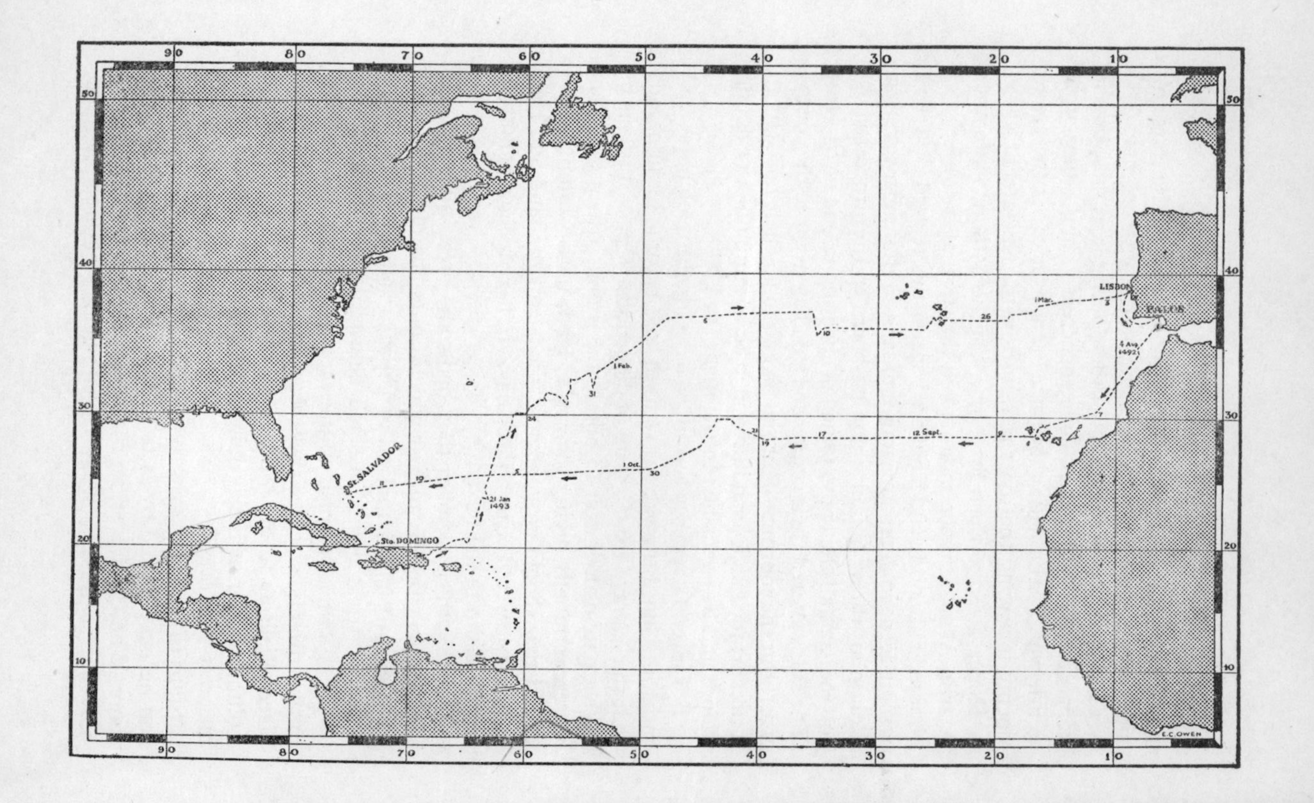
LISBON
PALOS
4 Aug
1492
1 Mar.
12 Sept.
1 Oct.
1 Feb.
21 Jan
1493
St. SALVADOR
Sta. DOMINGO
E.C. OWEN

horizon, they again broke forth into loud clamours, and insisted upon abandoning the voyage. Columbus endeavoured to pacify them by gentle words and liberal promises; but finding these only increased their violence, he assumed a different tone, and told them it was useless to murmur; the expedition had been sent by the sovereigns to seek the Indies, and happen what might, he was determined to persevere until, by the blessing of God, he should accomplish the enterprise.

He was now at open defiance with his crew, and his situation would have been desperate, but, fortunately, the manifestations of land on the following day were such as no longer to admit of doubt. A green fish, such as keeps about rocks, swam by the ships; and a branch of thorn, with berries on it, floated by; they picked up also a reed, a small board, and, above all, a staff artificially carved. All gloom and murmuring was now at an end, and throughout the day each one was on the watch for the long-sought land.

In the evening, when, according to custom, the mariners had sung the *Salve regina*, or vesper hymn to the Virgin Mary, Columbus made an impressive address to his crew, pointing out the goodness of God in thus conducting them by soft and favouring breezes across a tranquil ocean to the promised land. He expressed a strong confidence of making land that very night, and ordered that a vigilant lookout should be kept from the forecastle, promising to whomsoever should make the discovery a doublet of velvet, in addition to the pension to be given by the sovereigns.

The breeze had been fresh all day, with more sea than usual; at sunset they stood again to the west, and were ploughing the waves at a rapid rate, the *Pinta* keeping the lead for she was the faster ship.

The greatest animation prevailed throughout the ships; not an eye was closed that night. As the evening darkened, Columbus took his station on the top of the castle or cabin on the high poop of his vessel. It was to him a time of the most painful anxiety; he maintained an intense and unremitting watch, ranging his eye along the dusky horizon, in search of the most vague indications of land. Suddenly, about ten o'clock, he thought he beheld a light glimmering at a distance. Fearing that his eager hopes might deceive him, he called to Pedro Gutierrez, gentleman of the King's bedchamber, and demanded whether he saw a light in that direction. The latter replied in the affirmative. Columbus, yet doubtful whether it might not be some delusion of the fancy, called Rodrigo Sanchez of Segovia, and made the same inquiry, but by the time the latter had ascended the cabin the light had disappeared. They saw it once or twice afterwards in sudden and passing gleams, as if it were a torch in the bark of a fisherman, rising and sinking with the waves; or in the hands of some person on shore, borne up and down as he walked from house to house. So transient and uncertain were these gleams that few attached any importance to them; Columbus, however, considered them as certain signs of land, and, moreover, that the land was inhabited.

They continued on their course until two in the morning, when a gun from the *Pinta* gave the joyful signal of land. It was first discovered by a mariner named Rodriguez Bermejo, resident of Triana a suburb of Seville, but the reward was afterwards adjudged to the Admiral, for having previously perceived the light. The land was now clearly seen about two leagues distant, whereupon they took in sail, and laid to, waiting impatiently for the dawn.

The thoughts and feelings of Columbus in this little space of time must have been tumultuous and intense. At last, in spite of every difficulty and danger, he had accomplished his object. The great mystery of the ocean was revealed; his theory, which had been the scoff of sages, was triumphantly established; he had secured to himself a glory which must be as durable as the world itself.

It is difficult even for the imagination to conceive the feelings of such a man, at the moment of so sublime a discovery. What a bewildering crowd of conjectures must have thronged upon his mind, as to the land which lay before him, covered with darkness. That it was fruitful was evident from the vegetables which floated from its shores. He thought, too, that he perceived in the air the fragrance of aromatic groves. The moving light which he had beheld proved that it was the residence of man. But what were its inhabitants?

Were they like those of other parts of the globe, or were they some strange and monstrous race, such as the imagination in those times was prone to give to all remote and unknown regions? Had he come upon some wild island, far in the Indian seas; or was this the famed Cipango itself, the object of his golden fancies? A thousand speculations of this kind must have swarmed upon him, as he watched for the night to pass away; wondering whether the morning light would reveal a savage wilderness, or dawn upon spicy groves and glittering temples and gilded cities, and all the splendours of oriental civilisation.

It was the 12th of October.

CHAPTER II

FIRST LANDING OF COLUMBUS—CRUISING AMONG THE BAHAMA ISLANDS—DISCOVERY OF CUBA AND HAITI—THE BUILDING OF THE FORTRESS OF LA NAVIDAD.

WHEN the day dawned, Columbus saw before him a level and beautiful island, several leagues in extent, of great freshness and verdure, and covered with trees like a continual orchard. Though everything appeared in the wild luxuriance of untamed nature, the island was evidently populated, for the inhabitants were seen issuing from the woods, and running from all parts to the shore. They were all perfectly naked, and, from their attitudes and gesture, appeared lost in astonishment at the sight of the ships. Columbus made signal to cast anchor, and to man the boats. He entered his own boat richly attired in scarlet, and bearing the royal standard. Martin Alonzo Pinzon, and Vicente Yañez, his brother, likewise put off in their boats, each bearing the banner of the enterprise, emblazoned with a green cross, having on each side the letters F and Y, surmounted by crowns, the Spanish initials of the Castilian monarchs, Ferdinand (Fernando) and Isabella (Ysabel).

As they approached the shores they were delighted by the beauty and grandeur of the forests; the variety of unknown fruits on the trees which overhung the shores; the purity of the atmosphere, and the crystal transparency of the seas which bathe these islands. On landing, Columbus threw himself upon his knees, kissed the earth, and returned thanks to God with tears of joy. His example was followed by his companions, whose breasts, indeed, were full to overflowing. Columbus, then rising, drew his sword, displayed the royal standard, and took possession, in the names of the Castilian sovereigns, giving the island the name of San Salvador[1]. He then called upon all present to take the oath of obedience to him, as Admiral and Viceroy, and representative of the sovereigns.

His followers now burst forth into the most extravagant joy. They thronged around him, some embracing him, others kissing his hands. Those who had been most mutinous and turbulent during the voyage, were now most devoted and enthusiastic. Some begged favours of him, as of a man who had already wealth and honours in his gift. Many abject spirits, who had outraged him by their insolence, now crouched at his feet, begging his forgiveness, and offering, for the future, the blindest obedience to his commands.

The natives of the island, when, at the dawn of day, they had beheld the ships hovering on the coast, had supposed them some monsters, which had issued from the deep during the night. Their veering about, without any apparent effort, and the shifting and furling of their sails, resembling huge wings, filled them with astonishment. When they beheld the boats approach the shore, and a number of strange beings, clad in glittering steel, or raiment of various colours, landing upon the beach, they fled in fright to their woods. Finding, however, that there was no attempt to pursue or molest them, they gradually recovered from their terror, and approached the Spaniards with great awe, frequently prostrating themselves, and making signs of adoration. During the ceremony of taking possession they remained gazing, in timid admiration, at the complexion, the beards, the shining armour, and splendid dress of the Spaniards. The Admiral particularly attracted their attention, from his commanding height, his air of authority, his scarlet dress, and the deference paid to him by his companions; all which pointed him out to be the commander.

When they had still further recovered from their fears they approached the Spaniards, touched their beards, and examined their hands and faces, admiring their whiteness. Columbus, pleased with their simplicity, their gentleness, and the confidence they reposed in beings who must have appeared so

[1] Now known as Watlings Island.

strange and formidable, submitted to their scrutiny with perfect acquiescence. The wondering savages were won by this graciousness; they now supposed that the ships had sailed out of the crystal firmament which bounded their horizon, or that they had descended from above, on their ample wings, and that these marvellous beings were inhabitants of the skies.

The natives of the island were no less objects of curiosity to the Spaniards, differing, as they did, from any race of men they had ever seen. They were entirely naked, and painted with a variety of colours and devices, so as to have a wild and fantastic appearance. Their natural complexion was of a tawny, or copper hue, and they were entirely destitute of beards. Their hair was not crisped, like the recently discovered tribes of Africa under the same latitude, but straight and coarse, partly cut above the ears, but some locks behind left long, and falling upon their shoulders. Their features, though disfigured by paint, were agreeable; they had lofty foreheads and remarkably fine eyes. They were of moderate stature and well shaped; most of them appeared to be under thirty years of age. There was but one female with them, quite young, naked like her companions, and beautifully formed.

Their only arms were lances, hardened at the end by fire, or pointed with a flint or the bone of a fish. There was no iron to be seen among them, nor did they know its properties, for when a drawn sword was presented to them they unguardedly took it by the edge. Columbus distributed among them coloured caps, glass beads, hawk's bells, and other trifles, which they received as inestimable gifts and, decorating themselves with them, were delighted with their finery.

As Columbus supposed himself to have landed on an island at the extremity of India, he called the natives by the general appellation of Indians, which was universally adopted before the nature of his discovery was known, and has since been extended to all the aboriginals of the New World. The Spaniards remained all day on shore, refreshing themselves, after their anxious voyage, amidst the beautiful groves of the island,

and they returned to their ships late in the evening, delighted with all they had seen.

The island where Columbus had thus, for the first time, set his foot upon the New World, is one of the Bahama Islands, and was called by the natives Guanahani.

On the following morning, at daybreak, some of the natives came swimming to the ships, and others came in light canoes, formed of a single tree, hollowed, and capable of holding from between one and forty or fifty men. The Spaniards soon discovered that they were destitute of wealth, and had little to offer in return for trinkets, except balls of cotton yarn and domesticated parrots. They brought cakes of a kind of bread called cassava, made from the *yucca* root, which constituted a principal part of their food.

The avarice of the discoverers was awakened by perceiving small ornaments of gold in the noses of some of the natives. On being asked where this precious metal was procured, they answered by signs, pointing to the south, and Columbus understood them to say that a king resided in that quarter, of such wealth that he was served in great vessels of gold. He interpreted all their imperfect communications according to his previous ideas and his cherished wishes. They spoke of a warlike people, who often invaded their island from the northwest, and carried off the inhabitants. These he concluded to be the people of the mainland of Asia, subjects of the Grand Khan, who, according to Marco Polo, were accustomed to make war upon the islands and make slaves of the natives. The rich country to the south could be no other than the island of Cipango, and the king who was served out of golden vessels must be the monarch whose magnificent palace was said to be covered with plates of gold.

Having explored the island and taken in a supply of wood and water, Columbus set sail in quest of the opulent country to the south, taking seven of the natives with him, to acquire the Spanish language, and serve as interpreters and guides.

He now beheld a number of beautiful islands, green, level, and fertile, and the Indians intimated by signs that they were innumerable; he supposed them to be a part of the great archipelago described by Marco Polo as stretching along the coast of Asia, and abounding with spices and trees. He visited three of them, to which he gave the names of Santa Maria de la Conception, Fernandina, and Isabella. The inhabitants gave the same proofs as those of San Salvador of being totally unaccustomed to the sight of civilized man. They regarded the Spaniards as superhuman beings, approached them with offerings, of whatever their poverty, or rather, their simple and natural mode of life, afforded; the fruits of their fields and groves, their cotton yarn, and their domesticated parrots. When the Spaniards landed in search of water they took them to the coolest springs, the sweetest and freshest runs, filling their casks, and seeking in every way to gratify their celestial visitors.

Columbus was enchanted by the lovely scenery of some of these islands. "I know not," says he, "where first to go, nor are my eyes ever weary of gazing on the beautiful verdure. The singing of the birds is such that it seems as if one would never desire to depart hence. There are flocks of parrots that obscure the sun, and other birds of many kinds, large and small, entirely different from ours. Trees, also, of a thousand species, each having its particular fruit, and all of marvellous flavour. I believe there are many herbs and trees which would be of great value in Spain for tinctures, medicines, and spices, but I know nothing of them which gives me great vexation."

The fish which abounded in these seas partook of the novelty which characterized most of the objects in this new world. They rivalled the birds in the tropical brilliancy of their colours, the scales of some of them glanced back the rays of light like precious stones, and as they sported about the ships they flashed gleams of gold and silver through the crystal waves.

Columbus was disappointed in his hopes of finding any gold or spices in these islands; but the natives continued to point to the south as the region of wealth, and began to speak of an island in that direction, called Cuba, which, the Spaniards understood them to say, abounded in gold, pearls, and spices, carried on an extensive commerce, and that large merchant ships came to trade with the inhabitants. Columbus concluded this to be the desired Cipango, and the merchant ships to be those of the Grand Khan. He set sail in search of it, and after being delayed for several days, by contrary winds and calms, among the small islands of the Bahama bank and channel, he arrived in sight of it on the 28th of October.

As he approached this island he was struck with its magnitude, the grandeur of its mountains, its fertile valleys and long, sweeping plains, covered by stately forests and watered by noble rivers. He anchored in a beautiful river to the west of Nuevitas del Principe, and taking formal possession of the island, gave it the name of Juana, in honour of Prince Juan, and to the river the name of San Salvador.

Columbus spent several days coasting this part of the island and exploring the fine harbours and rivers with which it abounds. From his continual remarks in his *Journal* on the beauty of the scenery, and from the pleasure which he evidently derived from rural sounds and objects, he appears to have been extremely open to those delicious influences exercised over some spirits by the graces and wonders of nature. He was, in fact, in a mood to see everything through a fond and favouring medium, for he was enjoying the fulfilment of his hopes, the hard-earned but glorious reward of his toils and perils, and it is difficult to conceive the rapturous state of his feelings while thus exploring the charms of a virgin world, won by his enterprise and valour.

NOVEMBER

He frequently deceived himself in fancying that he heard the song of the nightingale, a bird unknown in these countries. From the grass growing to the very edge of the water he inferred the peacefulness of the ocean which bathes these islands, never lashing the shores with angry surges. Since his arrival among these Antilles he had experienced nothing but soft and gentle weather, and he concluded that a perpetual serenity reigned over these seas, little suspicious of the occasional bursts of fury to which they are liable, and to the tremendous hurricanes which rend and devastate the face of nature.

While coasting the island he landed occasionally and visited the villages, the inhabitants of which fled to the woods and mountains. The houses were constructed of branches of palm-trees, and were scattered under the spreading trees, like tents in a camp. They were better built than those he had hitherto visited, and extremely clean. He found in them rude images and wooden masks, carved with considerable ingenuity. Finding implements for fishing in all the cabins, he concluded that the coasts were inhabited merely by fishermen, who supplied the cities in the interior.

After coasting to the northwest for some distance Columbus came in sight of a great headland, to which, from the groves which covered it, he gave the name of the Cape of Palms. Here he learned that behind this bay there was a river, from whence it was but four days' journey to Cubanacan. By this name the natives designated a province in the centre of Cuba; *nacan* in their language signifying, in the midst. Columbus fancied, however, that they were talking of Cublai Khan, the Tartar sovereign, and understood them to say that Cuba was not an island, but terra firma. He concluded that this must be a part of the mainland of Asia, and that he could be at no great distance from Cathay, the ultimate destination of his voyage. The prince said to reign over the neighbouring country might be some oriental potentate of consequence; he determined, therefore, to send a present to him, and one of his letters of recommendation from the Castilian sovereigns.

For this purpose he chose two Spaniards, one of whom was a converted Jew, and knew Hebrew, Chaldaic, and a little Arabic, one or other of which languages, it was thought, must be known to this oriental prince. Two Indians were sent with them as guides; they were furnished with strings of beads and various trinkets, for their travelling expenses, and enjoined to inform themselves accurately concerning the situation of certain provinces, ports, and rivers of Asia, and to ascertain whether drugs and spices abounded in the country. The ambassadors penetrated twelve leagues into the interior, when they came to a village of fifty houses, and at least a thousand inhabitants. They were received with great kindness, conducted to the principal house, and provisions placed before them after which the Indians seated themselves on the ground around their visitors, and waited to hear what they had to communicate.

The Israelite found his Hebrew, Chaldaic, and Arabic of no avail, and the Lucayen interpreter had to be the orator. He made a speech after the Indian manner, extolling the power, wealth, and munificence of the white men. When he had finished, the Indians crowded round the Spaniards, touched and examined their skin and raiment, and kissed their hands and feet in token of adoration. There was no appearance of gold, or any other article of great value, among them; and when they were shown specimens of various spices they said there was nothing of the kind to be found in the neighbourhood, but far off to the southwest.

Finding no traces of the city and court they had anticipated, the envoys returned to their ships; on the way back they beheld several of the natives going about with firebrands in their hands, and certain dried herbs, which they rolled up in a leaf, and lighting one end, put the other in their mouths, and continued inhaling and puffing out the smoke. A roll of this kind they called a tobacco. The Spaniards were struck with astonishment at this singular, and apparently preposterous luxury.

The report of the envoys put an end to many splendid fancies of Columbus about this barbaric Prince and his capital; all that they had seen betokened a primitive and simple state of society; the country, though fertile and beautiful, was wild, and but slightly and rudely cultivated; the people were evidently strangers to civilised man, nor could they hear of any inland city superior to the one they had visited.

As fast as one illusion passed away, however, another succeeded. Columbus now understood from the signs of the Indians that there was a country to the eastward where the people collected gold along the river banks by torchlight, and afterwards wrought it into bars with hammers. In speaking of this place they frequently used the words Babeque and Bohio, which he supposed to be the names of islands or provinces. The cool nights gave hints of approaching winter, and he resolved not to proceed further to the north, and turning eastward, sailed in quest of Babeque, which he trusted might prove some rich and civilised island.

After running along the coast for two or three days, and passing a great cape, to which he gave the name of Cape Cuba, he stood out to sea in the direction pointed out by the Indians. The wind, however, came directly ahead, and after various ineffectual attempts he had to return to Cuba. What gave him great uneasiness was that the *Pinta*, commanded by Martin Alonzo Pinzon, parted company with him during this attempt. She was the best ship, and had worked considerably to windward of the others. Pinzon paid no attention to the signals of Columbus to turn back, though they were repeated at night by lights at the masthead; when morning dawned, the *Pinta* was no longer to be seen.

Columbus considered this a wilful desertion, and was much troubled and perplexed by it. Martin Alonzo had for some time shown impatience at the domination of the Admiral. He was a veteran navigator, of great abilities, and accustomed from his wealth and standing to give the law among his nautical associates. He had furnished two of the ships and much of the funds for the expedition, and thought himself entitled to an equal share in the command. Several disputes therefore, had occurred between him and the Admiral. Columbus feared he might have departed to make an independent cruise, or might have the intention to hasten back to Spain, and claim the merit of the discovery. These thoughts distracted his mind, and embarrassed him in the further prosecution of his discoveries.

For several days he continued exploring the coast of Cuba, until he reached the eastern end, and to which, from supposing it the extreme point of Asia, he gave the name of Alpha and Omega, the beginning and the end. While steering at large beyond this cape, undetermined which course to take, he saw high mountains towering above the clear horizon to the southeast, and giving evidence of an island of great extent. He immediately sailed to it, to the great consternation of his Indian guides, who continued to assure him by various signs that the inhabitants had but one eye, and were cannibals.

In the transparent atmosphere of the tropics, objects are descried at a great distance, and the purity of the air and serenity of the deep blue sky give a magical charm to scenery. Under these advantages, the beautiful island of Haiti revealed itself to the eye as they approached. Its mountains were higher and more rocky than those of the other islands, but the rocks rose from among rich forests. The mountains swept down into luxuriant plains and green savannas, while the appearance of cultivated fields, with the numerous fires at night, and the columns of smoke which rose in various parts by day, all showed it to be populous. It rose before them in all the splendour of tropical vegetation, one of the most beautiful islands in the world, and doomed to be one of the most unfortunate.

During the evening of the 6th of December, Columbus entered a harbour at the western end of the island, to which he gave the name of St. Nicolas, by which it is called at the present day. Columbus continued along the northern coastline, anchoring occasionally in some of the many fine natural harbours, one of which he called Conception. Here the sailors caught several kinds of fish similar to those of their own country; they heard also the notes of a bird which sings in the night, and which they mistook for the nightingale. The features of the surrounding country so resembled those of the more beautiful provinces of Spain that the Admiral named the island Española, or, as it is commonly written, Hispaniola.

DECEMBER

During his travels along this northern coastline of Haiti, Columbus visited many of the caciques and received numerous kindnesses, and learned much of the customs and habits of the local inhabitants.

On Christmas day, due to the laxity of his crew and treacherous currents which run swiftly along the coast, his ship was carried on to a sandbank. Efforts were made to lighten her by cutting away the mast, but in vain. The keel was firmly embedded in the sand; the seams opened, and the breakers beat against her until she fell over on one side. The Admiral abandoned the wreck, and took refuge with his men on board the caravel. He laid-to until daylight, sending messengers on shore to inform the cacique, Guacinagari, of his disastrous ship wreck.

When the chieftain heard of the misfortune of Columbus he assembled his people and salvaged the wreck. It was here that Columbus decided to establish a fortress to which he gave the name, La Navidad, or the Nativity—a memorial of his having been preserved from the wreck of his ship on Christmas day.

CHAPTER III

RETURN VOYAGE—VIOLENT STORMS—ARRIVAL AT PORTUGAL—VISIT TO THE COURT OF PORTUGAL—ARRIVAL AT PALOS.

IT was on the 4th of January 1493 that Columbus set sail from La Navidad, on his return to Spain. On the 6th, along the coast, a sailor at the masthead cried out that there was a sail at a distance, standing towards them. To their great joy it proved to be the *Pinta*, which came sweeping before the wind with flowing canvas. On joining the Admiral, Pinzon endeavoured to excuse his desertion by saying that he had been separated from him by stress of weather, and had ever since been seeking him. Columbus ascertained, afterwards, that Pinzon had parted company intentionally, and had steered directly east, in quest of a region where the Indians on board of his vessel had assured him he would find gold in abundance. They had guided him to Hispaniola, where he had been for some time in a river about fifteen leagues east of La Navidad, trading with the natives. He had collected a large quantity of gold, one-half of which he retained as captain, the rest he divided among his men to secure their secrecy and fidelity. On leaving the river he had carried off four Indian men and two girls, to be sold in Spain.

JANUARY

Columbus sailed for this river, to which he gave the name of Rio de Gracia, but it long continued to be known as the river of Martin Alonzo. Here he ordered the four men and two girls to be dismissed, well clothed and with many presents, to atone for the wrong they had experienced, and to allay the hostile feeling it might have caused among the natives. This restitution was not made without great unwillingness and many angry words on the part of Pinzon.

Columbus, on leaving the river, took four young Indians to guide him to the Caribbean Islands, situated to the east, of which they gave him very interesting accounts, as well as of the island of Mantinino, said to be inhabited by Amazons. A favourable breeze sprang up, however, for the voyage homewards, and, seeing gloom and impatience in the countenances of his men at the idea of diverting from their route, he gave up his intention of visiting these islands for the present, and made sail for Spain.

FEBRUARY

The trade winds, which had been so propitious on the outward voyage, were equally adverse to a return. The favourable breeze soon died away; light winds from the east, and frequent calms, succeeded, but they had intervals of favourable weather, and by the 12th of February they had made such progress as to begin to flatter themselves with the hopes of soon beholding land. The wind now came on to blow violently; on the following evening there were three flashes of lightning in the north-north-east, from which signs Columbus predicted an approaching tempest. It soon burst upon them with frightful violence; their small and crazy vessels were little fitted for the wild storms of the Atlantic; all night they were obliged to scud under bare masts at the mercy of the elements. As the morning dawned there was a transient pause, and they made a little headway, but the wind rose with redoubled fury from the south and increased in the night, the vessels labouring terribly in a cross sea, which threatened at each moment to overwhelm them or dash them to pieces. The tempest still augmenting, they were obliged again to scud before the wind. The Admiral made signal lights for the *Pinta* to keep in company; for some time she replied by similar signals, but she was separated by the violence of the storm; her lights gleamed more and more distant, until they ceased entirely. When the day dawned the sea presented a frightful waste of wild, broken waves, lashed into fury by the gale; Columbus looked round anxiously for the *Pinta*, but she was nowhere to be seen.

Throughout a dreary day the helpless bark was driven along

by the tempest. Seeing all human skill baffled and confounded, Columbus endeavoured to propitiate Heaven by solemn vows. Lots were cast to perform pilgrimages and penitences, most of which fell upon Columbus; among other things, he was to perform a solemn mass, and to watch and pray all night in the chapel of the convent of Santa Clara, at Moguer. Various private vows were made by the seamen, and one by the Admiral and the whole crew, that, if they were spared to reach the land, they would walk in procession, bare-footed, to offer up thanksgivings in some church dedicated to the Virgin Mary

The heavens, however, seemed deaf to all their vows; the storm grew still more furious, and every one gave himself up for lost. During this long and awful conflict of the elements, the mind of Columbus was a prey to the most distressing anxiety. He was harassed by the repinings of his crew, who cursed the hour of their leaving their country, and their want of resolution in not compelling him to abandon the voyage. But he had a source of great distress, more intolerable than death itself. It was highly probable that the *Pinta* had foundered in the storm. In such case, the history of his discovery would depend upon his own feeble bark, one surge of the ocean might bury it forever in oblivion, and his name only remain as that of a desperate adventurer, who perished in search of fanciful idea.

In the midst of these gloomy reflections an expedient suggested itself, by which, though he and his ships might perish, the glory of his achievement might survive to his name, and its advantages be secured to his sovereigns. He wrote on parchment a brief account of his discovery, and of his having taken possession of the newly found lands in the name of their Catholic majesties. This he sealed and directed to the King and Queen, and superscribed a promise of a thousand ducats to whomsoever should deliver the packet unopened. He then wrapped it in a waxed cloth, which he placed in the centre of a cake of wax, and inclosing the whole in a cask, threw it into the sea. A copy of this memorial he enclosed in a similar manner, and placed it upon the poop of his vessel, so that, should the caravel sink, the cask might float off and survive.

Happily, these precautions, though wise, were superfluous; at sunset there was a streak of clear sky in the west, the wind shifted to that quarter, and on the morning of the 15th of February they came in sight of land. The joy of the crew at once more beholding the old world was almost equal to those they had experienced on discovering the new. For two or three days, however, they remained hovering in sight of land, of which they only caught glimpses through the mist and rain. At length they came to anchor at the island of Santa Maria, the most southern of the Azores, and a possession of the crown of Portugal. An ungenerous reception, however, awaited the poor, tempest-tossed mariners, on their return to the abode of civilised man, far different from the kindness and hospitality they had experienced among the savages of the New World. Columbus had sent one-half of the crew on shore, to fulfill the vow of a barefooted procession to a hermitage or chapel of the Virgin, which stood on a solitary part of the coast, and awaited their return to perform the same ceremony with the remainder of his crew. Scarcely had they begun their prayers and thanksgiving, when a party of horse and foot, headed by the governor of the island, surrounded the hermitage and took them all prisoners. The real object of this outrage was to get possession of the person of Columbus; for the King of Portugal, jealous lest his enterprise might interfere with his own discoveries, had sent orders to his commanders of islands and distant ports to seize and detain him wherever he should be met with.

Having failed in this open attempt, the governor next endeavoured to get Columbus in his power by stratagem, but was equally unsuccessful. A violent altercation took place between them, and Columbus threatened him with the vengeance of his sovereigns. At length, after two or three days' detention, the sailors who had been captured in the chapel were released; the governor pretended to have acted through doubts of Columbus having a regular commission, but that being now convinced of his being in the service of the Spanish sovereigns, he was ready to yield him every service in his power. The Admiral did not put his offers to the proof. The wind became favourable for the continuation of his voyage, and he again set sail, on the 24th of February. After two or three days of pleasant sailing there was a renewal of tempestuous weather. About mid-

MARCH

night of the 2nd of March the caravel was struck by a squall, which rent all her sails, and threatened instant destruction. The crew were again reduced to despair, and made vows of fastings and pilgrimages. The storm raged throughout the succeeding day, during which, from various signs, they considered themselves in the vicinity of land, which they supposed must be the coast of Portugal. The turbulence of the following night was dreadful. The sea was broken, wild, and mountainous, the rain fell in torrents, and the lightning flashed and the thunder pealed from various parts of the heavens.

In the first watch of this fearful night the seamen gave the usually welcome cry of land, but it only increased their alarm, for they were ignorant of their situation, and dreaded being driven on shore or dashed upon the rocks. Taking in sail, therefore, they endeavoured to keep to sea as much as possible. At daybreak on the 4th of March they found themselves off the rock of Cintra, at the mouth of the Tagus. Though distrustful of the goodwill of Portugal, Columbus had no alternative but to run in for shelter, and he accordingly anchored about three o'clock in the river, opposite to Rastello. The inhabitants came off from various parts of the shore, to congratulate him on what they deemed a miraculous preservation, for they had been watching the vessel the whole morning with great anxiety, and putting up prayers for her safety. The oldest mariners of the place assured him that they had never known so tempestuous a winter. Such were the difficulties and perils with which Columbus had to contend on his return to Europe; had one-tenth of them seen him sail on his outward voyage, his factious crew would have risen in arms against the enterprise, and he never would have discovered the New World.

Immediately on his arrival in the Tagus, Columbus despatched a courier to the King and Queen of Spain, with tidings of his discovery. He wrote also to the King of Portugal, entreating permission to go to Lisbon with his vessel, as a report had got abroad that she was laden with gold, and he felt himself insecure in the neighbourhood of a place like Rastello, inhabited by needy and adventurous people. At the same time he stated the route and events of his voyage, lest the King should suspect him of having been in the route of the Portuguese discoveries.

The tidings of this wonderful bark, freighted with the people and productions of a newly discovered world, filled all Lisbon with astonishment. For several days the Tagus was covered with barges and boats going to and from it. Among the visitors were various officers of the crown, and cavaliers of high distinction. All hung with rapt attention upon the accounts of the voyage, and gazed with insatiable curiosity upon the plants and animals, and, above all, upon the inhabitants of the New World. The enthusiasm of some, and the avarice of others, was excited, while many repined at the incredulity of the King and his counsellors, by which so grand a discovery had been forever lost to Portugal.

On the 8th of March Columbus received a message from King John, congratulating him upon his arrival, and inviting him to the court at Valparaiso, about nine leagues from Lisbon. The King at the same time ordered that anything which the Admiral required for himself or his vessel should be furnished free of cost.

Columbus distrusted the good faith of the King, and set out reluctantly for the court; but his reception was what might have been expected from an enlightened and liberal king. On approaching the royal residence he was met by the principal personages of the King's household, and conducted with great ceremony to the palace. The King welcomed him to Portugal, and congratulated him on the glorious result of his enterprise. He ordered him to seat himself in his presence, an honour only granted to persons of royal dignity, and assured him that everything in his kingdom was at the service of his sovereigns and himself. They had repeated conversations about the events of the voyage, and the King made minute inquiries as to the soil, productions, and people of the newly discovered countries, and the routes by which Columbus had sailed. The King listened with seeming pleasure to his replies, but was secretly grieved at the thought that this splendid enterprise had been offered to him and refused. He was uneasy, also, lest this undefined discovery should in some way interfere with his own territories, comprehended in the papal bull[1] which granted to the crown of Portugal all the lands it should discover from Cape Non to the Indies.

On suggesting these doubts to his counsellors, they eagerly encouraged them, for some of them were the very persons who had scoffed at Columbus as a dreamer, and his success covered them with confusion. They declared that the colour, hair, and manners of the natives brought in the caravel agreed exactly with the descriptions given of the people of that part of India granted to Portugal by the papal bull. Others observed that there was but little distance between the Terceira Islands and those which Columbus had discovered; the latter, therefore, clearly belonged to Portugal. Others endeavoured to awaken the anger of the King, by declaring that Columbus had talked in an arrogant tone of his discovery, merely to revenge himself upon the monarch for having rejected his propositions.

Seeing the King deeply perturbed in spirit, some even went so far as to propose, as an effectual means of impeding the prosecution of these enterprises, that Columbus should be assassinated.

Happily, the King had too much magnanimity to adopt such wicked and dastardly counsel. Though secretly grieved and mortified that the rival power of Spain should have won this triumph which he had rejected, yet he did justice to the great merit of Columbus, and honoured him as a distinguished benefactor to mankind. He felt it his duty, also, as a generous prince, to protect all strangers driven by adverse fortune to his ports. Others of his council advised that he should secretly fit out a powerful armament, and dispatch it, under guidance of two Portuguese mariners who had sailed with Columbus, to take

[1] See page 52.

possession of the newly discovered country; he might then settle the question of right with Spain by an appeal to arms. This counsel, in which there was a mixture of courage and craft, was more relished by the King, and he resolved to put it promptly in execution.

In the meantime Columbus was escorted back to his ship by a numerous train of cavaliers of the court, and on the way paid a visit to the Queen at a monastery of San Antonio at Villa Franca, where he was listened to with wonder, as he related the events of his voyage to her majesty and the ladies of her court. The King had offered him a free passage by land to Spain, at the royal expense, but as the weather had moderated, he preferred to return in his caravel[1]. Putting to sea on the 13th of March, therefore, he arrived safely at Palos on the 15th, having taken not quite seven and a half months to accomplish this most momentous of all maritime enterprises.

The triumphant return of Columbus was a prodigious event in the little community of Palos, every member of which was more or less interested in the fate of the expedition. Many had lamented their friends as lost, while imagination had lent mysterious horrors to their fate. When, therefore, they beheld one of the adventurous vessels furling her sails in their harbour, from the discovery of a world, the whole community broke forth into a transport of joy, the bells were rung, the shops shut, and all business suspended. Columbus landed, and walked in procession to the church of St. George, to return thanks to God for his safe arrival.

Understanding that the court was at Barcelona, he at first felt disposed to proceed there in the caravel, but, reflecting on the dangers and disasters of his recent voyage, he gave up the idea, and dispatched a letter to the sovereigns, informing them of his arrival. He then departed for Seville to await their reply. It arrived within a few days, and was as gratifying as his heart could have desired. The sovereigns were dazzled and astonished by this sudden and easy acquisition of a new empire of indefinite extent, and apparently boundless wealth. They addressed

[1] The *Santa Maria* was wrecked and left at Haiti.

Columbus by his titles of Admiral and Viceroy, promising him still greater rewards, and urging him to repair immediately to court to concert plans for a second and more extensive expedition.

It is fitting here to speak a word of the fate of Martin Alonzo Pinzon. By a singular coincidence, which appears to be well authenticated, he anchored at Palos on the evening of the same day that Columbus had arrived. He had been driven by the storm into the Bay of Biscay, and had made the port of Bayonne. Doubting whether Columbus had survived the tempest, he had immediately written to the sovereigns, giving an account of the discovery, and requesting permission to come to court and relate the particulars in person. As soon as the weather was favourable he again set sail, anticipating a triumphant reception in his native port of Palos. When, on entering the harbour, he beheld the vessel of the Admiral riding at anchor, and learned the enthusiasm with which he had been received, his heart died within him.

It is said that he feared to meet Columbus in this hour of his triumph, lest he should put him under arrest for his desertion on the coast of Cuba; but this is not likely, for he was a man of too much resolution to yield to such a fear. It is more probable that a consciousness of his misconduct made him unwilling to appear before the public in the midst of their enthusiasm for Columbus, and to witness the honours heaped upon a man whose superiority he had been so unwilling to acknowledge. Whatever may have been his motive, it is said that he landed privately in his boat, and kept out of sight until the departure of the Admiral, when he returned to his home broken in health, and deeply dejected, awaiting the reply of the sovereigns to his letter. The reply at length arrived, forbidding his coming to court, and severely reproaching him for his conduct. This letter completed his humiliation; the wounds of his feelings gave virulence to his bodily malady, and in a few days he died, a victim to grief and repentance. Let no one, however, indulge in harsh censures over Pinzon. His merits and services are entitled to the highest praise; his errors should be regarded with indulgence. He was one of the first in Spain to appreciate the project of Columbus, aiding him with money when poor and unknown at Palos. He afterwards enabled him to procure and fit out his ships, when even the mandates of the sovereigns were ineffectual; and finally he embarked in the expedition with his brothers and friends, staking life, property, everything, upon the event.

He had thus entitled himself to participate largely in the glory of this immortal enterprise when, unfortunately, forgetting for a moment the grandeur of the cause and the implicit obedience due to the commander, he yielded to the incitements of self-interest, and was guilty of that act of insubordination which has cast a shade upon his name. Much may be said, however, in extenuation of his fault; his consciousness of having rendered great services to the expedition and of possessing property in the ships, and his habits of command which rendered him impatient of control.

That he was a man naturally of generous sentiments and honorable ambition is evident from the poignancy with which he felt the disgrace drawn upon him by his conduct. A mean man would not have fallen a victim to self-upbraiding for having been convicted of a mean action. His story shows how one lapse from duty may counterbalance the merits of a thousand services; how one moment of weakness may mar the beauty of a whole life of virtue; and how important it is for a man, under all circumstances, to be true, not merely to others, but to himself.

CHAPTER IV

RECEPTION OF COLUMBUS IN SPAIN—TO THE COURT AT BARCELONA—PAPAL BULL OF PETITION.

THE journey of Columbus to Barcelona was like the progress of a sovereign. Wherever he passed, the surrounding country poured forth its inhabitants, who lined the road and thronged the villages, rending the air with acclamations. In the large towns the streets, windows, and balconies were filled with spectators, eager to gain a sight of him, and of the Indians whom he carried with him, who were regarded with as much astonishment as if they had been natives of another planet.

APRIL

It was about the middle of April that he arrived at Barcelona, and the beauty and serenity of the weather, in that genial season and favoured climate, contributed to give splendour to the memorable ceremony of his reception. His entrance into this noble city has been compared to one of those triumphs which the Romans were accustomed to decree to conquerors. First were paraded the six Indians, painted according to their savage fashion, and decorated with their ornaments of gold. After these were borne various kinds of live parrots, together with stuffed birds and animals of unknown species, and rare plants supposed to be of precious qualities; while special care was taken to display the Indian coronets, bracelets, and other decorations of gold, which might give an idea of the wealth of the newly discovered regions. After this followed Columbus, on horseback, surrounded by a brilliant cavalcade of Spanish chivalry. The streets were almost impassable from the multitude; the houses, even to the very roofs, were crowded with spectators. It seemed as if the public eye could not be sated with gazing at these trophies of an unknown world, or on the remarkable man by whom it had been discovered. There was a sublimity in this event that mingled a solemn feeling with the public joy.

To receive him with suitable distinction the sovereigns had ordered their throne to be placed in public, under a rich canopy of brocade of gold, where they awaited his arrival, seated in state, with Prince Juan beside them, and surrounded by their principal nobility. Columbus arrived in their presence, accompanied by a brilliant crowd of cavaliers, among whom, we are told, he was conspicuous for his stately and commanding person, which, with his venerable grey hairs, gave him the august appearance of a senator of Rome. On his approach the sovereigns rose, as if receiving a person of the highest rank, and ordered him to seat himself in their presence—a rare honour in this proud and punctilious court.

He now gave an account of the most striking events of his voyage, and displayed the various productions and the native inhabitants which he had brought from the new world. He assured their majesties that all these were but harbingers of greater discoveries which he had yet to make, which would add realms of incalculable wealth to their dominions.

When Columbus had finished, the King and Queen sank on their knees, raised their hands to heaven, and, with eyes filled with tears of joy and gratitude, poured forth thanks and praises to God. All present followed their example; a deep and solemn enthusiasm pervaded that splendid assembly and prevented all common acclamations of triumph. The anthem of *Te Deum laudamus* was chanted by the choir of the royal chapel. Such was the solemn and pious manner in which the brilliant court of Spain celebrated this sublime event; offering up a grateful tribute of melody and praise, and giving glory to God for the discovery of another world.

During his sojourn at Barcelona the sovereigns took every occasion to bestow on Columbus the highest marks of personal consideration. He was admitted at all times to the royal presence; appeared occasionally with the King on horseback, riding on one side of him, while Prince Juan rode on the other side; and the Queen delighted to converse familiarly with him on the subject of his voyage. To perpetuate in his family the glory of his achievement a coat of arms was given him, in which he was allowed to quarter the royal arms, the castle and lion, with those more particularly assigned him, which were a group of islands surrounded by waves; to these arms was afterwards annexed the motto:

A CASTILLA Y A LEON
NUEVO MUNDO DIO COLON.
(To Castile and Leon
Columbus gave a new world.)

The pension of thirty crowns, which had been decreed by the sovereigns to whomsoever should first discover land, was adjudged to Columbus, for having first seen the light on the shore.

The favour shown Columbus by the sovereigns insured him for a time the caresses of the nobility; for, in a court, every one is eager to lavish attentions upon the man "whom the King delights to honour". At one of the banquets which were given him occurred the well-known circumstance of the egg[1]. A shallow courtier present, impatient of the honours paid to Columbus, and meanly jealous of him as a foreigner, abruptly asked him whether he thought that, in case he had not discovered the Indies, there would have been wanting men in Spain capable of the enterprise. To this Columbus made no direct reply, but, taking an egg, invited the company to make it stand upon one end. Every one attempted it, but in vain; whereupon he struck it upon the table, broke one end, and left it standing on the broken part; illustrating, in this simple manner, that when he had once shown the way to the New World nothing was easier than to follow it.

The joy occasioned by this great discovery was not confined to Spain; the whole civilised world was filled with wonder and delight. Every one rejoiced in it as an event in which he was more or less interested, and which opened a new and unbounded field for inquiry and enterprise. Men of learning and science

[1] This story is doubted by many modern historians.

shed tears of joy, and those of ardent imaginations indulged in the most extravagant and delightful dreams. Notwithstanding all this triumph, however, no one had an idea of the real importance of the discovery. The opinion of Columbus was universally adopted, that Cuba was the end of the Asiatic continent, and that the adjacent islands were in the Indian Seas. They were called, therefore, the West Indies, and as the region thus discovered appeared to be of vast and indefinite extent, and existing in a state of nature, it received the comprehensive appellation of "the New World".

In the midst of their rejoicings the Spanish sovereigns lost no time in taking every measure to secure their new acquisitions. During the crusades a doctrine had been established among the Christian princes, according to which the Pope, from his supreme authority over all temporal things, as Christ's vicar on earth, was considered as empowered to dispose of all heathen lands to such Christian potentates as would undertake to reduce them to the dominion of the Church, and to introduce into them the light of religion.

Alexander the Sixth, a native of Valencia, and born a subject to the crown of Arragon, had recently been elevated to the papal chair. Ferdinand dispatched ambassadors to him, announcing the new discovery as an extraordinary triumph of the faith, and a vast acquisition of empire to the Church. He took care to state that it did not in the least interfere with the possessions ceded by the Holy Chair to Portugal, all which had been sedulously avoided; he supplicated his Holiness, therefore, to issue a bull, granting to the crown of Castile dominion over all those lands, and such others as might be discovered in those parts, artfully intimating, at the same time, his determination to maintain possession of them however his Holiness might decide.

A bull was accordingly issued, dated May 2, 1493, investing the Spanish sovereigns with similar rights, privileges, and indulgences, in respect to the newly discovered regions, to those granted to the Portuguese with respect to their African discoveries, and under the same condition of propagating the

Catholic faith. To prevent any conflicting claims, however, between the two powers, the famous line of demarcation was established. This was an ideal line drawn from the north to the south pole, a hundred leagues west of the Azores and the Cape de Verde Islands. All land discovered by the Spanish navigators to the west of this line was to belong to the crown of Castile; all land discovered in the contrary direction was to belong to Portugal.

SECOND VOYAGE, 1493

CHAPTER V

PREPARATIONS FOR A SECOND VOYAGE—DEPARTURE FROM SPAIN—DISCOVERY OF THE CARIBBEAN ISLANDS—TO HAITI—FOUNDING OF THE CITY OF ISABELLA—IN SEARCH OF GOLD

THE utmost exertions were now being made to fit out the second expedition of Columbus. To insure regularity and dispatch in the affairs relative to the New World, they were placed under the superintendence of Juan Rodriguez de Fonseca, Archdeacon of Seville. Francisco Pinelo was associated with him as treasurer, and Juan de Soria as comptroller. Their office was fixed at Seville, and was the germ of the Royal India house, which rose to such great power and importance. No one was permitted to embark for the newly discovered lands without express license from either the sovereigns, Columbus, or Fonseca.

MAY

As the conversion of the heathen was professed to be the grand object of these discoveries, twelve ecclesiastics were chosen to accompany the expedition, at the head of whom was Bernardo Buyl, or Boyle, a Benedictine monk, a man of talent and reputed sanctity, and a subtle politician. He was appointed by the Pope his apostolical vicar for the New World. These monks were charged by Isabella with the spiritual instruction of the Indians, and provided by her with all things necessary for the dignified performance of the rites and ceremonies of the Church. The Queen had taken a warm and compassionate interest in the welfare of the natives, looking upon them as committed by Heaven to her peculiar care. She gave general orders that they should be treated with the utmost kindness, and enjoined Columbus to inflict signal punishment on all Spaniards who should wrong them. The six Indians brought by the Admiral to Barcelona were baptised with great state and solemnity, the King, the Queen, and Prince Juan officiating as sponsors, and were considered as an offering to Heaven of the first fruits of these pagan nations.

The preparations for the expedition were quickened by the proceedings of the court of Portugal. John the Second, unfortunately for himself, had among his counsellors certain politicians of that short-sighted class who mistake craft for wisdom. By adopting their perfidious policy he had lost the New World when it was an object of honourable enterprise; in compliance with their advice, he now sought to retrieve it by subtle strategy. A large armament was fitting out, the avowed object of which was an expedition to Africa, but its real destination to seize upon the newly discovered countries. To lull suspicion, he sent ambassadors to the Spanish court to congratulate the sovereigns on the success of Columbus, and to amuse them with negotiations respecting their discoveries. Ferdinand had received early intelligence of the naval preparations of Portugal, and perfectly understood the real purpose of this mission. A keen diplomatic game ensued between the sovereigns, wherein the parties were playing for a newly discovered world. Questions and propositions were multiplied and entangled; the object of each being merely to gain time to dispatch his expedition.

By the indefatigable exertions of Columbus, aided by Fonseca and Soria, a fleet of seventeen, large and small, were soon in a state of forwardness; labourers and artificers of all kinds were engaged for the projected colony; and an ample supply was provided of whatever was necessary for its subsistence and defence, for the cultivation of the soil, the working of the mines, and the traffic with the natives.

The extraordinary excitement which prevailed respecting this expedition, and the magnificent ideas which were entertained concerning the New World, drew volunteers of all kinds to Seville. It was a romantic and stirring age, and the Moorish wars being over, the bold and restless spirits of the nation were in want of suitable employment. Many hidalgos of high rank, officers of the royal household and Andalusian cavaliers, pressed into the expedition, some in the royal service, others at their own cost, fancying they were about to enter upon a glorious career of arms, in the splendid countries and among the semi-barbarous nations of the East.

Among the noted personages who engaged in the expedition was a young cavalier of a good family, named Don Alonzo de Ojeda, who deserves particular mention. He was small, but well proportioned and muscular, of a dark but handsome and animated countenance, and possessed of incredible strength and agility. He was expert at all kinds of weapons, accomplished in all manly and warlike exercises, an admirable horseman, and a partisan soldier of the highest order. Bold of heart, free of spirit, open of hand; fierce in fight, quick in brawl, but ready to forgive and prone to forget an injury; he was for a long time the idol of the rash and roving youth who engaged in the early expeditions to the New World, and distinguished himself by many perilous enterprises and singular exploits.

During the fitting out of the armament, various disputes occurred between Columbus and the persons appointed by the Crown to assist him. Juan de Soria, the comptroller, demurred occasionally to the expenses, which exceeded the amount originally calculated, and he sometimes refused to sign the accounts of the Admiral. The Archdeacon Fonseca, also, disputed the requisitions of Columbus for footmen and domestics suitable to his state as Viceroy. They both received reprimands from the sovereigns, and were commanded to study in everything the wishes of Columbus. From this trifling cause we may date the rise of an implacable hostility, ever after manifested by Fonseca towards Columbus.

SEPTEMBER

The departure of Columbus on his second voyage of discovery presented a brilliant contrast to his gloomy embarkation at Palos. On the 25th of September, at the dawn of day, the Bay of Cadiz was whitened by his fleet. There were three large ships of heavy burden, and fourteen caravels. The number of persons permitted to embark had originally been limited to one thousand, but many volunteers were allowed to enlist without pay, others got on board of the ships by stealth, so that eventually about fifteen hundred set sail in the fleet. All were full of animation, and took a gay leave of their friends, anticipating a prosperous voyage and triumphant return. Instead of being regarded by the populace as devoted men, bound upon a dark and desperate enterprise, they were contemplated with envy as favoured mortals, destined to golden regions and delightful climes, where nothing but wealth and wonder and enjoyment awaited them. Columbus moved among the throng and wherever he passed, every eye followed him with admiration, and every tongue extolled and blessed him. Before sunrise the whole fleet was under way; the weather was serene and propitious, and as the populace watched their parting sails brightening in the morning beams, they looked forward to their joyful return, laden with the treasures of the New World.

Columbus touched at the Canary Islands, where he took in wood and water, and procured live stock, plants, and seeds, to be propagated in Hispaniola. On the 13th of October he lost sight of the island of Ferro, and, favoured by the trade winds, was borne pleasantly along, shaping his course to the southwest, hoping to fall in with the islands of the Caribs, of which he had received such interesting accounts in his first voyage. At the dawn of day of the 2nd of November a lofty island was descried to the west, to which he gave the name of Dominica, from having discovered it on Sunday. As the ships moved gently onward other islands rose to sight, one after another, covered with forests, and enlivened by flights of parrots and other tropical birds, while the whole air was sweetened by the fragrance of the breezes which passed over them. These were a part of that beautiful cluster of islands called the Antilles, which sweep almost in a semi-circle from the eastern end of Porto Rico to Paria, on the coast of Venezuela, forming a kind of barrier between the main ocean and the Caribbean Sea. In

OCTOBER

NOVEMBER

one of those islands, to which they gave the name of Guadaloupe, the Spaniards first met with the delicious anana, or pineapple.

After leaving Guadaloupe, Columbus touched at other of the Caribbean Islands. At one of them which he named Santa Cruz, a ship's boat, sent on shore for water, had an encounter with a canoe, in which were a few Indians, two of whom were females. The women fought as desperately as the men, and plied their bows with such vigour, that one of them sent an arrow through a Spanish buckler, and wounded the soldier who bore it. The canoe being run down and overset, they continued to fight while in the water, gathering themselves occasionally on sunken rocks, and managing their weapons as dexterously as if they had been on firm ground. It was with the utmost difficulty they could be overpowered and taken.

Pursuing his voyage, Columbus passed by a cluster of small islands, to which he gave the name of The Eleven Thousand Virgins, and arrived one evening in sight of a great island, covered with fine forests, and indented with havens. It was called by the natives Boriquen, but he named it San Juan Bautista; it is now known by the name of Porto Rico. After running for a whole day along its beautiful coast, and touching at a bay at the west end, he arrived, on the 22nd of November, off the eastern extremity of Haiti, or Hispaniola. Passing by the gulf of Las Fleches, Columbus set on shore one of the young Indians who had been taken from the neighbourhood, and had accompanied him to Spain. He dismissed him finely apparelled and loaded with trinkets, anticipating favourable effects from the accounts he would be able to give to his countrymen of the power and munificence of the Spaniards, but he never heard anything more of him. Only one Indian of those who had been to Spain remained in the fleet, a young Lucayan, native of the island of Guanahani, who had been baptised at Barcelona, and named after the Admiral's brother, Diego Colon; he continued always faithful and devoted to the Spaniards.

Continuing along the coast, Columbus paused in the neighbourhood of Monte Christi, to fix upon a place for a settlement, in the neighbourhood of a stream said to abound in gold, to which, in his first voyage, he had given the name of Rio del Oro.

On the evening of the 27th of November Columbus anchored opposite to the harbour of La Navidad and found the fortress built during the first voyage burnt and destroyed.

Columbus searched for a place for a projected colony, and fixed upon a harbour about ten leagues east of Monte Christi, protected on one side by a natural rampart of rocks, and on the other by an impervious forest, with a fine plain in the vicinity, watered by two rivers. A great inducement, also, for settling here, was, that it was at no great distance from the mountains of Cibao, where the gold mines were situated.

The troops and the various persons to be employed in the colony were immediately disembarked, together with the stores, arms, ammunition, and all the cattle and live stock. An encampment was formed on the margin of the plain, round a sheet of water, and the plan of a town traced out, and the houses commenced. The public edifices, such as a church, a storehouse, and a residence for the Admiral, were constructed of stone, the rest of wood, plaster, reeds, and such other materials as could be readily procured. Thus was founded the first Christian city of the New World, to which Columbus gave the name of Isabella, in honour of his royal patroness.

For a time every one exerted himself with zeal; but maladies soon began to make their appearance. Many had suffered from sea-sickness, and the long confinement on board of the ships; others, from the exposures on the land, before houses could be built for their reception. The important and hurried labours of building the city and cultivating the earth bore hard upon the Spaniards, many of whom were unaccustomed to labour, and needed repose and relaxation. The maladies of the mind also mingled with those of the body. Many, as has been shown, had embarked in the enterprise with the most visionary and romantic expectations. What, then, was their surprise at finding themselves surrounded by impracticable forests, doomed to toil painfully for mere subsistence, and to attain every comfort by the severest exertion! As to gold, which they had expected to find readily and in abundance, it was to be procured only in small quantities, and by patient and persevering labour. All these disappointments sank deep into their hearts, their spirits flagged as their golden dreams melted away, and the gloom of despondency aided the ravages of disease. Columbus himself was overcome by the fatigues, anxieties, and exposures he had suffered, and for several weeks was confined to his bed by severe illness; but his energetic mind rose superior to the maladies of the body, and he continued to give directions about the building of the city, and the general concerns of the expedition.

The greater part of the ships were ready to return to Spain, but he had no treasure to send with them. It was necessary for him to do something before the vessels sailed, to keep up the reputation of his discoveries, and justify his own magnificent representations. The region of the mine lay at a distance of three or four days' journey, directly in the interior; the very name of the cacique, Caonabo, signifying "the lord of the golden house", seemed to indicate the wealth of his dominions. Columbus determined, therefore, to send an expedition to explore them. If the result should answer to the accounts given by the Indians, he would be able to send home the fleet with confidence, bearing tidings of the discovery of the golden mountains of Cibao.

The person chosen for this enterprise was Alonzo de Ojeda, who delighted in any task of an adventurous nature. He set out from the harbour early in January, 1494, accompanied by a small number of well-armed men, several of them young and spirited cavaliers like himself. They crossed the first range of mountains by a narrow and winding Indian path, and descended into a vast plain, covered with noble forests, and studded with villages and hamlets. The inhabitants overwhelmed them with hospitality, and delayed them in their journey by their kindness. They had to ford many rivers, so that they were six days in reaching the chain of mountains which locked up, as it were, the golden

JANUARY, 1494

region of Cibao. Here they saw ample signs of natural wealth. The sands of the mountain streams glittered with particles of gold; in some places they picked up large specimens of virgin ore, and stones streaked and richly impregnated with it. Ojeda, himself, found a mass of rude gold in one of the brooks, weighing nine ounces.

The little band returned to the harbour, with enthusiastic accounts of the golden promise of these mountains. A young cavalier, named Gorvalan, who had been sent to explore a different tract of country, returned with similar reports. Encouraged by these good tidings, Columbus lost no time in dispatching twelve of the ships, under the command of Antonio de Torres, retaining only five for the service of the colony. By these ships he sent home specimens of the gold found among the mountains of Cibao, and of all fruits and plants of unknown and valuable species, together with the Carib captives, to be instructed in the Spanish language and the Christian faith, that they might serve as interpreters, and aid in the conversion of their countrymen. He wrote, also, a sanguine account of the two expeditions into the interior, and expressed a confident expectation, as soon as the health of himself and his people would permit, of procuring and making abundant shipments of gold, spices, and valuable drugs. He extolled the fertility of the soil, evinced in the luxuriant growth of the sugar cane, and of various European grains and vegetables; but entreated supplies of provisions for the immediate wants of the colony, as their stores were nearly exhausted, and they could not accustom themselves to the diet of the natives.

When the fleet arrived in Europe, though it brought no great quantities of gold, the tidings from Columbus and his companions kept up the popular excitement. There was something wonderfully grand in the idea of introducing new races of animals and plants, of building cities, extending colonies, and sowing the seeds of civilisation and of enlightened empire in this beautiful but savage world. It struck the minds of learned and classical men with admiration, and filled them with pleasant dreams.

But while such pleasant anticipations were indulged in Europe, murmuring and sedition began to prevail among the colonists. Disappointed in their hopes of wealth, disgusted with the labours imposed upon them, and appalled by prevalent sickness, they looked with horror upon the surrounding wilderness, and became impatient to return to Spain. Their discontents were increased by one Firmin Cado, who had come out as assayer and purifier of metals, but whose ignorance in his art equalled his obstinacy of opinion. He insisted that there was scarcely any gold in the island, and that all the specimens brought by the natives had been accumulated in the course of several generations, and been handed down from father to son in their families.

At length a conspiracy was formed, headed by Bernal Diaz de Pisa, the comptroller, to take advantage of the illness of Columbus, to seize upon the ships remaining in the harbour, and to return to Spain; where they thought it would be easy to justify their conduct by accusing Columbus of gross deceptions and exaggerations concerning the countries he had discovered. Fortunately, Columbus received information in time, and arrested the ringleaders of the conspiracy. Bernal Diaz was confined on board one of the ships, to be sent to Spain for trial; and several of the inferior mutineers were punished, but not with the severity their offence deserved. This was the first time Columbus exercised the right of punishing delinquents in his new government, and it immediately caused a great clamour against him. Already the disadvantage of being a foreigner was clearly manifested. He had no natural friends to rally round him; whereas the mutineers had connections in Spain, friends in the colony, and met with sympathy in every discontented mind.

CHAPTER VI

EXPEDITION INTO THE INTERIOR

AS the surest means of quieting the murmurs and rousing the spirits of his people, Columbus, as soon as his health permitted, made preparations for an expedition to the mountains of Cibao, to explore the country, and establish a post in the vicinity of the mines. Placing his brother Diego in command at Isabella, during his absence, and taking with him every person in health that could be spared from the settlement, and all the cavalry, he departed, on the 12th of March, at the head of four hundred men, armed with helmets and corselets, with arquebuses, lances, swords, and crossbows, and followed by labourers and miners, and a multitude of the neighbouring Indians. After traversing a plain and fording two rivers, they encamped in the evening at the foot of a wild and rocky pass of the mountains.

MARCH

The ascent of this defile presented formidable difficulties to the little army, which was encumbered with various munitions and with mining implements. There was nothing but an Indian footpath, winding among rocks and precipices, and the entangled vegetation of a tropical forest. A number of high-spirited young cavaliers, therefore, threw themselves in the advance, and aiding the labourers and pioneers, and stimulating them with promises of liberal reward, they soon constructed the first road formed by Europeans in the New World, which, in commemoration of their generous zeal, was called *El Puerto de los Hidalgos*, or the Pass of the Hidalgos.

On the following day the army toiled up this steep defile, and arrived where the gorge of the mountain opened into the interior. Here a glorious prospect burst upon their view. Below lay a vast and delicious plain, with all the rich variety of tropical vegetation. Palms of prodigious height and spreading mahogany trees towered from amid a wilderness of the foliage. Universal freshness and verdure were maintained by numerous streams which meandered gleaming through the woodland, while various villages and hamlets seen among the trees, and the smoke of others rising out of the forests, gave signs of a numerous population. The luxuriant landscape extended as far as the eye could see, until it appeared to melt away and mingle with the horizon. The Spaniards gazed with rapture upon this soft, voluptuous country, which seemed to realise their ideas of an earthly paradise, and Columbus struck with its vast extent, gave it the name of *Vega Real*, or Royal Plain.

Having descended the rugged pass, the army issued upon the plain in military array, with a great noise of warlike instruments. When the Indians beheld this band of warriors, glittering in steel, emerging from the mountains, and heard, for the first time, their rocks and forests echoing to the din of drum and trumpet, they were bewildered with astonishment. The horses especially excited their terror and admiration.

For two or three days their march continued. They crossed two large rivers: one, called the Yagui by the natives, was named by the Admiral the River of Reeds; to the other he gave the name of *Rio Verde*, or Green River, from the verdure and freshness of its banks. At length they arrived at a chain of lofty and rugged mountains which formed a kind of barrier to the vega, and amidst which lay the golden region of Cibao. On entering, instead of the soft, luxuriant landscape of the vega, nothing was to be seen but chains of rocky and sterile mountains, scantily clothed with pines. The very name of the country bespoke the nature of the soil, Cibao, in the language of the natives, signifying a stone. But what consoled the Spaniards for the asperity of the soil was to observe particles of gold among the sands of the streams, which they regarded as earnests of the wealth locked up in the mountains.

Choosing a situation in a neighbourhood that seemed to abound in mines, Columbus began to build a fortress, to which he gave the name of St. Thomas, intended as a pleasant, though pious, reproof of Firmin Cado and his doubting adherents, who had refused to believe that the island contained gold until they should behold it with their eyes and touch it with their hands.

While the Admiral remained superintending the building of the fortress he dispatched a young cavalier of Madrid, named Juan de Luxan, with a small band of armed men to explore the province. Luxan returned after a few days, with the most satisfactory accounts. He found many parts of Cibao more capable of cultivation than those that had been seen by the Admiral. The forests appeared to abound with spices; the trees were overrun with vines bearing clusters of grapes of pleasant flavour; while every valley and glen had its stream, yielding more or less gold, and showing the universal prevalence of that precious metal.

The natives of the surrounding country likewise flocked to the fortress of St. Thomas, bringing gold to exchange for European trinkets. One old man brought two pieces of virgin ore weighing an ounce, and thought himself richly repaid on receiving a hawk's bell. On observing the admiration of the Admiral at the size of these specimens, he assured him that in his country, which lay at half a day's distance, pieces were found as big as an orange. Others spoke of masses of ore as large as the head of a child, to be met with in their neighbourhood. As usual, however, these golden tracts were always in some remote valley, or along some rugged and sequestered stream; and the wealthiest spot was sure to lie at the greatest distance—for the land of promise is always beyond the mountain.

The fortress of St. Thomas being nearly completed, Columbus left it in command of Pedro Margarite, with a garrison of fifty-six men, and set out on his return to Isabella. He paused for a time in the vega to establish routes between the fortress and the harbour; during which he sojourned in the villages, that his men might become accustomed to the food of the natives, and that a mutual good-will might grow up between them.

As we accompany Columbus, in imagination, on his return to the harbour, over the rocky height from whence the vega first broke upon the eye of the Spaniards, we cannot help pausing to cast back a look of mingled pity and admiration over this beautiful but devoted region. The dream of natural liberty and ignorant content was as yet unbroken; the white man had penetrated into the land; avarice and pride and ambition, and sordid care and pining labour, were soon to follow, and the indolent paradise of the Indian was about to disappear forever.

CHAPTER VII

SICKNESS AND DISCONTENT AMONG THE SPANIARDS—COLUMBUS PREPARES FOR A VOYAGE TO CUBA—THE DISCOVERY OF JAMAICA—ILLNESS OF COLUMBUS—HE MEETS HIS BROTHER BARTHOLOMEW AT HAITI—TROUBLES ON THE ISLAND—INTRIGUES AGAINST COLUMBUS IN SPAIN.

COLUMBUS had scarcely returned to the harbour, when a messenger arrived from Pedro Margarite, the commander at Fort St. Thomas, informing him that the Indians of the vicinity had abandoned their villages and broken off all intercourse, and that he understood the chief, Caonabo, was assembling his warriors to attack the fortress. From what the Admiral had seen of the Indians in the interior, and the awe in which they stood of the white men he felt little apprehensions from their hostility, and contented himself with sending a reinforcement of twenty men to the fortress, and detaching thirty more to open the road between it and the port.

Columbus was, at this time, planning a voyage to explore the coast of Cuba, but it was indispensable before sailing, to place the affairs of the island in such a state as to insure tranquility. For this purpose he determined to send all the men that could be spared from the concerns of the city, or the care of the sick, into the interior, where they could be subsisted among the natives, and become accustomed to their diet. A little army was accordingly mustered of two hundred and fifty crossbow-men, one hundred and ten arquebusiers, sixteen horsemen, and twenty officers. These were to be commanded by Pedro Margarite, while Ojeda was to succeed him in the command of Fort St. Thomas.

Columbus wrote a long and earnest letter of instructions to

Margarite, desiring him to make a military tour, and to explore the principal parts of the island; but enjoining on him the strictest discipline of his army, and the most vigilant care to protect the rights of the Indians, and cultivate their friendship. Ojeda set off at the head of the little army for the fortress; on his way he learnt that three Spaniards had been robbed of their effects by five Indians at the ford of one of the rivers of the vega, and that the delinquents had been sheltered by their cacique, who had shared their booty. Ojeda was a quick and an impetuous soldier, whose ideas were all of a military kind. He seized one of the thieves, ordered his ears to be cut off in the public square of the village, and sent the cacique, with his son and nephew, in chains to the Admiral, who, after terrifying them with preparation for a public execution, pretended to yield to the tears and entreaties of their friends, and set them at liberty.

Having thus distributed his forces about the island, and taken measures for its tranquillity, Columbus formed a junta for its government, of which his brother Don Diego was president, and Father Boyle, Pedro Fernandez Coronal, Alonzo Sanchez Caravajal, and Juan de Luxan, were counsellors. Leaving in the harbour two of his largest ships, which drew too much water to explore unknown coasts and rivers, he set sail on the 24th of April, with the *Niña*, the *San Juan*, and the *Cordera*.

APRIL

The plan of the present expedition of Columbus was to revisit Cuba at the point where he had abandoned it on his first voyage, and thence to explore it on the southern side. As has already been observed, he supposed it to be a continent, and the extreme end of Asia; and if so, by following its shores in the proposed direction, he trusted to arrive at Cathay, and other rich and commercial, though semi-barbarous countries, forming part of the territories of the Grand Khan, as described by Mandeville and Marco Polo.

The plan of the present expedition of Columbus was to revisit Cuba, to which in his preceding voyage he had given the name of Alpha and Omega, but which is now known as P. de Maysi, he sailed along the southern coast, touching once or twice in the harbours. The natives crowded to the shores, gazing with astonishment at the ships as they glided gently along at no great distance. They held up fruits and other provisions, to tempt the Spaniards to land, while others came off in canoes, offering various refreshments, not in barter, but as free gifts. On inquiring of them for gold, they uniformly pointed to the south, intimating that a great island lay in that direction, where it was to be found in abundance. On the 3rd of May, therefore, Columbus turned his prow directly south, and, abandoning the coast of Cuba for a time, steered in quest of this reported island. He had not sailed many leagues before the blue summits of Jamaica began to rise above the horizon. It was two days and a night, however, before he reached it, filled with admiration, as he gradually drew near, at its vast extent, the beauty of its mountains, the majesty of its forests, and the great number of villages which animated the whole face of the country.

MAY

He coasted the island from about the centre to a port at the western end, which he called the Gulf of Buentiempo, known today as Montego Bay. He found the natives more ingenious as well as more warlike than those of Cuba and Haiti. Their canoes were constructed with more art, and ornamented at the bow and stern with carving and painting. Many were of great size, though formed of the hollow trunks of single trees, often a species of the mahogany. Columbus measured one which proved to be ninety-six feet long and eight broad; it was hollowed out of one of those magnificent trees which rise like verdant towers amidst the rich forests of the tropics. Every cacique possessed a large canoe of the kind, which he seemed to regard as his galley of state. The Spaniards at first were treated with hostility, and were compelled to skirmish with the natives, but a friendly intercourse succeeded.

Columbus being disappointed in his hopes of finding gold in Jamaica, and the breeze being fair for Cuba, he decided to return.

Having steered again for Cuba, Columbus, on the 18th of May, arrived at a great cape, to which he gave the name of

Cabo de la Cruz[1], which it still retains. Coasting to the west, he soon got entagled in a complete labyrinth of small islands and keys; some of them were low, naked, and sandy, others covered with verdure, and others tufted with lofty and beautiful forests. To this archipelago, which extended as far as the eye could reach, and, in a manner, enamelled the face of the ocean with variegated verdure, he gave the name of the Queen's Garden. He persuaded himself that these were the islands mentioned by Sir John Mandeville and Marco Polo, as fringing the coast of Asia; if so, he must soon arrive at the dominions of the Grand Khan.

There was much in the character of the scenery to favour the idea. As the ships glided along the smooth and glassy channels which separated the islands, the magnificence of their vegetation, the soft odours wafted from flowers and blossoms and aromatic shrubs, the splendid plumage of scarlet cranes, flamingoes, and other tropical birds, and the gaudy clouds of butterflies, all resembled those described of oriental climes.

Emerging from the labyrinth of the Queen's Garden, Columbus pursued his voyage with a prosperous breeze along that part of the southern side of Cuba where, for nearly thirty-five leagues, the navigation is free from banks and islands; to his left was the broad and open sea, whose dark blue colour gave token of ample depth; to his right extended a richly wooded country, called Ornofay, with noble mountains, frequent streams, and numerous villages. The appearance of the ships spread wonder and joy along the coast. The natives came off swimming or in canoes, to offer fruits and other presents. After the usual evening shower, when the breeze blew from the shore and brought off the sweetness of the land, it bore with it also the distant songs of the natives, and the sound of their crude music, as they were probably celebrating, with their national chants and dances, the arrival of these wonderful strangers on their coasts.

Animated by the delusions of his fancy, Columbus continued

[1] This is the only name given by Columbus to any part of Cuba that has survived the present day.

to follow up this supposed continent of Asia; plunging into another wilderness of keys and islets towards the western end of Cuba, and exploring that perplexed and lonely coast.

In this navigation he had to contend with almost incredible difficulties and perils; his vessels having to be warped through narrow and shallow passages, where they frequently ran aground. He was encouraged to proceed by information which he received, or fancied he received, from the natives concerning a country farther on called Mangon, where the people wore clothing, and which he supposed must be Mangi, the rich Asiatic province described by Marco Polo. He also understood from them that among the mountains to the west there was a powerful king, who reigned in great state over many populous provinces; that he wore a white garment which swept the ground, that he was called a saint, and never spoke, but communicated his orders to his subjects by signs. In all this we see the busy imagination of Columbus interpreting the imperfectly understood communications of the Indians into unison with his preconceived ideas.

One day, a party being sent on shore for wood and water, while they were employed in cutting wood and filling their water-casks, an archer strayed into the forest with his crossbow, in search of game, but soon returned flying in breathless terror. He declared that he had seen through an opening glade a man dressed in long white robes, followed by two others in white tunics reaching to their knees, and that they had complexions as fair as Europeans.

Columbus was rejoiced at this intelligence, hoping that he had found the clothed inhabitants of Mangon. Two parties were dispatched, well armed, in quest of these people in white; the first returned unsuccessful; the other brought word of having tracked the footprints of some large animal with claws, supposed by them to have been either a lion or a griffin, but which most probably was an alligator. Dismayed at the sight, they hastened back to the sea. As no tribe of Indians wearing clothing was ever discovered in Cuba, it is probable the men in white were nothing else than a flock of cranes, seen by the wandering archer. These birds, like the flamingoes, feed in company, with one stationed at a distance as a sentinel. When seen through an opening of the woodlands, standing in rows in a shallow glassy pool, their height and erectness give them, at first glance, the semblance of human figures.

Columbus now hoped, by continuing on, to arrive ultimately at the *Aura Chersonesus* of the ancients; doubling which, he might make his way to the Red Sea, thence to Joppa, and so by the Mediterranean to Spain; or might circumnavigate Africa, pass triumphantly by the Portuguese as they were groping along the coast of Guinea, and after having thus circumnavigated the globe, furl his adventurous sails at the Pillars of Hercules, the *ne plus ultra* of the ancient world. But though his fellow-voyagers shared his opinion that they were coasting the continent of Asia, they were far from sharing his enthusiasm, and shrunk from the increasing perils of the voyage. The ships were strained and crazed by frequently running aground. The cables and rigging were much worn, the provisions nearly exhausted, and the crews worn out and disheartened by incessant labour. The Admiral, therefore, was finally persuaded to abandon all further prosecution of the voyage; but, before he turned back, he obliged the whole of the officers and seamen to sign a deposition, declaring their perfect conviction that Cuba was a continent, the beginning and the end of India. This singular instrument was signed near that deep bay called by some the Bay of Philipina, by others, —Cortes. At this very time a ship-boy from the masthead might have overlooked the group of islands to the south, and have beheld the open sea beyond. Had Columbus continued on for two or three days longer, he would have passed round the extremity of Cuba; his illusion would have been dispelled, and an entirely different course might have been given to his subsequent discoveries.

Returning now towards the east, the crews suffered excessively from fatigue and a scarcity of provisions. At length, on the 7th of July, they anchored at the mouth of a fine river, in a genial and abundant country, which

JULY

they had previously visited, as they had come down along the coast. Here the natives brought them provisions of various kinds. It was a custom with Columbus to erect crosses in all remarkable places, to denote the discovery of the country, and its subjugation to the true faith. This was done on the banks of this river, on a Sunday morning, with great ceremony. Columbus was attended by the cacique, and by his principal favourite, a venerable Indian, fourscore years of age. While Mass was performed in a stately grove, the natives looked on with awe and reverence. When it was ended, the old man of fourscore made a speech to Columbus in the Indian manner. "I am told," said he, "that thou hast lately come to these lands with a mighty force, and hast subdued many countries, spreading great fear among the people; but be not therefore vainglorious. Know that, according to our belief, the souls of men have two journeys to perform after they have departed from the body; one to a place dismal, foul, and covered with darkness, prepared for such as have been unjust and cruel to their fellow-men; the other full of delight, for such as have promoted peace on earth. If, then, thou art mortal, and dost expect to die, beware that thou hurt no man wrongfully, neither do harm to those who have done no harm to thee."

When this speech was explained to Columbus by his interpreter, he was greatly moved by the simple eloquence of this untutored savage, and rejoiced to hear his doctrine of a future state of the soul, having supposed that no belief of the kind existed among the inhabitants of these countries. He assured the old man that he had been sent by his sovereigns to teach them the true religion, to protect them from harm, and to subdue their enemies the Caribs. The venerable Indian was exceedingly astonished to learn that the Admiral, whom he had considered so great and powerful, was yet but a subject, and when he was told by the interpreter, who had been in Spain, of the grandeur of the Spanish monarchs, and of the wonders of their kingdom, a sudden desire seized him to embark with the Admiral, and accompany him to see this wonderful country, and it was only with extreme difficulty that his wife and children managed to dissuade him from his purpose.

After leaving this river, to which, from the solemn mass performed on its banks, Columbus gave the name of *Rio de la Misa*, he continued on to Cape Cruz, and then stood over to Jamaica, to complete the circumnavigation of that island. For nearly a month he continued beating to the eastward along its southern coast, coming to anchor every evening under the land, and making but slow progress. Anchoring one evening in a great bay, he was visited by a cacique with a numerous train, who remained until a late hour conversing with the Lucayan interpreter who had been in Spain, about the Spaniards and their country, and their prowess in vanquishing the Caribs.

On the following morning, when the ships were under way, they beheld three canoes issuing from among the islands of the bay. The centre one was large, and handsomely carved and painted. In it were seated the cacique and his family, consisting of two daughters, young and beautiful, two sons, and five brothers. They were all arrayed in their jewels, and attended by the officers of the chieftain, decorated with plumes, and mantles of variegated feathers. The standard-bearer stood in the prow with a fluttering white banner, while other Indians, fancifully painted, sounded trumpets of fine black wood ingeniously carved. The cacique, entering on board of the ship, distributed presents among the crew, and approaching the Admiral, "I have heard," said he, "of the irresistible power of thy sovereigns, and of the many nations thou hast subdued in their name. Thou hast destroyed the dwellings of the Caribs, slaying their warriors, and carrying their wives and children into captivity. All the islands are in dread of thee, for who can withstand thee, now that thou knowest the secrets of the land, and the weakness of the people? Rather, therefore, than thou shouldst take away my dominions, I will embark with all my household in thy ships, and will go to render homage to thy King and Queen, and behold thy country, of which I hear such wonders."

When this speech was interpreted to Columbus, and he beheld the wife, the sons, and daughters of the cacique, and considered to what ills they would be exposed, he was touched with compassion, and determined not to take them from their native land. He received the cacique under his protection, as a vassal of his sovereigns, but informed him that he had many lands yet to visit before he should return to his own country. He dismissed him, therefore, for the present, promising that at some future time he would gratify his wishes.

AUGUST

On the 19th of August Columbus lost sight of the eastern extremity of Jamaica, and on the following day made that long peninsula of Haiti, since called Cape Tiburon, but to which he gave the name of San Miguel. He coasted the whole of the southern side of the island, and had to take refuge in the channel of Saona from a violent storm which raged for several days, during which time he suffered great anxiety for the fate of the other vessels, which remained at sea, exposed to the fury of the tempest. Being rejoined by them, and the weather having moderated, he set sail eastward with the intention of completing the discovery of the Caribbee Islands, but his physical strength did not correspond to the efforts of his spirit. The extraordinary fatigues which he had suffered both in mind and body, during this harassing voyage, which had lasted for five months, had secretly preyed upon his health. He had shared in all the hardships and privations of the common seamen, and he had cares and trials from which they were exempt. When a sailor, worn out with the labours of his watch, slept soundly, in spite of the howling of the storms, the anxious commander maintained his painful vigil, through long, sleepless nights, amidst the pelting of the tempest and the drenching surges of the sea, for the safety of the ships depended upon his watchfulness. During a great part of the voyage he had been excited by the hope of soon arriving at the known parts of India; he was afterwards stimulated by a conflict with hardships and perils, as he made his way back against contrary winds and currents. The moment he was relieved from all solicitude, and found himself in a tranquil sea, which he had already explored, the excitement suddenly ceased, and mind and body sunk exhausted by almost superhuman exertions.

He fell into a deep lethargy, resembling death itself. His crew feared that death was really at hand. They abandoned, therefore, all farther prosecution of the voyage, and spreading their sails to a favourable breeze from the east, bore Columbus back, in a state of complete insensibility, to the harbour of Isabella.

A joyful and heartfelt surprise awaited Columbus on his arrival, in finding at his bedside his brother Bartholomew, the companion of his youth, his zealous coadjutor, and, in a manner, his second self, from whom he had been separated for several years.

Bartholomew had been away from Spain for about seven years, and reached Seville just as his brother had sailed; but being an accomplished navigator, the sovereigns gave him the command of three ships, freighted with supplies for the colony, and sent him to aid his brother in his enterprises. He again arrived too late, reaching the settlement of Isabella just after the departure of the Admiral for the coast of Cuba.

The sight of this brother was an inexpressible relief to Columbus, disabled as he was by sickness, overwhelmed with cares, and surrounded by strangers. His chief dependence had hitherto been upon his brother Don Diego; but the latter was of a mild and peaceable disposition, with an inclination for a clerical life, and was but little fitted to manage the affairs of a factious colony. Bartholomew was of a different and more efficient character. He was prompt, active, decided, and of a fearless spirit; whatever he determined he carried into instant execution, without regard to difficulty or danger. His body corresponded to his mind; he was tall, muscular, vigorous, and commanding. He had an air of great authority, but somewhat stern, wanting that sweetness and benignity which tempered the authoritative demeanor of the Admiral. Indeed, there was a certain asperity in his temper and a dryness and abruptness in his manners which made him many enemies; yet, notwithstanding these external defects, he was of a generous disposition, free from arrogance or malevolence, and as placable as he was brave.

He was a thorough seaman, both in theory and practice; he

was acquainted with Latin, but does not appear to have been highly educated, his knowledge, like that of his brother, being chiefly derived from a long course of varied experience and attentive observation, aided by the studies of maturer years. Equally vigorous and penetrating in intellect with the Admiral, but less enthusiastic in spirit and soaring in imagination, and with less simplicity of heart, he surpassed him in the adroit management of business, was more attentive to pecuniary interests, and had more of that worldly wisdom which is so important in the ordinary concerns of life. His genius might never have excited him to the sublime speculation which led to the discovery of a world, but his practical sagacity was calculated to turn that discovery to more advantage.

Anxious to relieve himself from the pressure of public business during his present sickness, Columbus immediately invested his brother with the title and authority of Adelantado, an office equivalent to that of Lieutenant-Governor. He felt the importance of his assistance in the present critical state of the colony, for during the few months that he had been absent the whole island had become a scene of violence and discord. A brief retrospect is here necessary, to explain the cause of this confusion.

Pedro Margarite, to whom Columbus on his departure had given orders to make a military tour of the island, set forth on his expedition with the greater part of the forces, leaving Alonzo de Ojeda in command of Fort St. Thomas. Instead, however, of proceeding on his tour, Margarite lingered among the populous and hospitable villages of the vega, where he and his soldiery, by their licentious and oppressive conduct, soon roused the indignation and hatred of the natives. Tidings of their excesses reached Don Diego Columbus, who, with the concurrence of the council, wrote to Margarite, reprehending his conduct, and ordering him to depart on his tour. Margarite replied in a haughty and arrogant tone, pretending to consider himself independent in his command, and above all responsibility to Don Diego or his council. He was supported in his tone of defiance by the kind of aristocratical party composed of the idle cavaliers of the colony, who had been deeply wounded in the *pundonor*, and affected to look down with contempt upon the newly coined nobility of Don Diego, and to consider Columbus and his brothers mere mercenary and upstart foreigners. In addition to these partisans Margarite had a powerful ally in his fellow-countryman, Friar Boyle, the apostolical vicar for the New World, an intriguing man, who had conceived a violent hostility against the Admiral, and had become disgusted with his mission to the wilderness.

A cabal was soon formed of most of those who were disaffected to the Admiral, and discontented with their abode in the colony. Margarite and Friar Boyle acted as if possessed of paramount authority; and, without consulting Don Diego or the council, took possession of certain ships in the harbour, and set sail for Spain, with their adherents. They were both favourites of the king, and deemed it would be an easy matter to justify their abandonment of their military and religious commands, by a pretended zeal for the public good, and a desire to represent to the sovereigns the disastrous state of the colony, and the tyranny and oppression of Columbus and his brothers. Thus the first general and apostle of the New World set the flagrant example of unauthorised abandonment of their posts.

The departure of Margarite left the army without a head; the soldiers now roved about in bands, or singly, according to their caprice, indulging in all kinds of excesses.

The arrival of four ships about this time, commanded by Antonio Torres, bringing out a physician and apothecary, various mechanics, millers, and husbandmen, and an ample supply of provisions, diffused universal joy among the suffering Spaniards. Columbus received a highly flattering letter from his sovereigns, approving of all that he had done, informing him that all differences with Portugal had been amicably adjusted, and inviting him to return to Spain, or to send some able person in his place, furnished with maps and charts, to be present at a convention for adjusting the dividing line of discovery between the two powers. Columbus hastened the return of the ships, sending his brother Diego to attend the convention, and to counteract the misrepresentations which he was aware had been sent home of his conduct, and which would be enforced by Margarite and Friar Boyle. He remitted, by the ships, all the gold he could collect, with specimens of fruits and valuable plants, and five hundred Indian captives, to be sold as slaves in Seville. It is painful to find the glory of Columbus sullied by such violations of the laws of humanity, but the customs of the times must plead his apology.

CHAPTER VIII

ARRIVAL FROM SPAIN OF AGUADO—DISCOVERY OF GOLD —COLUMBUS PLANS RETURN TO SPAIN.

WHILE Columbus was endeavouring to remedy the evils produced by the misconduct of Margarite and his followers, Margarite and his politic coadjutor Friar Boyle, were busily undermining his reputation in the court of Spain. They accused him of deceiving the sovereigns and the public by extravagant descriptions of the countries he had discovered; and of tyranny and oppression towards the colonists, compelling excessive labour during a time of sickness and debility; inflicting severe punishments for the most trifling offence, and heaping indignities on Spanish gentlemen of rank. They said nothing, however, of the exigencies which had called for unusual labour; nor of the idleness and profligacy of the commonalty, which called for coercion and chastisement; nor of the contumacy and cabals of the cavaliers, who had been treated with indulgence rather than severity. These representations, being supported by many factious and discontented idlers who had returned from the colony, and enforced by people of rank connected with the cavaliers, had a baneful effect upon the popularity of Columbus, and his favour with the sovereigns.

APRIL

About this time a measure was adopted which shows the declining influence of the Admiral. A proclamation was made on the 10th of April, giving general permission to native-born subjects to settle in the island of Hispaniola, and to go on private voyages of discovery and traffic to the New World. They were to pay certain proportions of their profits to the Crown, and to be subject to certain regulations. The privilege of an eighth part of the tonnage was likewise secured to Columbus, as Admiral; but he felt himself

SANTA MARIA

Spanish Caravel in which Columbus discovered America. From a drawing attributed to Columbus and placed in "The Epistola Christofori Columbi"—undated 8vo. Edition (?1494).

exceedingly aggrieved at this permission being granted without his knowledge or consent, considering it an infringement of his rights, and a measure likely to disturb the course of regular discovery by the licentious enterprises of reckless adventurers.

The arrival of the ships commanded by Torres, bringing accounts of the voyage along the southern coasts of Cuba, supposed to be the continent of Asia, and specimens of the gold and the vegetable and animal productions of the country, counterbalanced in some degree these unfavourable representations of Margarite and Boyle. Still it was determined to send out a commissioner to inquire into the alleged distress of the colony and the conduct of Columbus, and one Juan Aguado was appointed for the purpose. He had already been to Hispaniola, and on returning had been strongly recommended to royal favour by Columbus. In appointing a person, therefore, for whom the Admiral appeared to have a regard, and who was under obligations to him, the sovereigns thought, perhaps, to soften the harshness of the measure.

As to the five hundred slaves sent home in the ships of Torres, Isabella ordered a consultation of pious theologians to determine whether, having been taken in warfare, their sale as slaves would be justifiable in the sight of God. Much difference of opinion arose among the divines on this important question; whereupon the Queen decided it according to the dictates of her conscience and her heart, and ordered that the Indians should be taken back to their native country.

AUGUST

Juan de Aguado set sail from Spain towards the end of August, with four caravels freighted with supplies, and Don Diego Columbus returned in this squadron to Hispaniola. Aguado was one of those weak men whose heads are turned by the least elevation. Though under obligations to Columbus, he forgot them all, and forgot even the nature and extent of his own commission. Finding Columbus absent in the interior of the island, on his arrival, he acted as if the reins of government had been transferred into his hands. He paid no respect to Don Bartholomew, who had been placed in command by his brother during his absence, but proclaiming his letter of credence by sound of trumpet, he proceeded to arrest various public officers, to call others to rigorous account, and to invite every one who had wrongs or grievances to complain of, to come forward boldly and make them known. He already regarded Columbus as a criminal, and intimated, and perhaps thought, that he was keeping at a distance through fear of his investigations. He even talked of setting off to arrest him. The whole community was in confusion; it was considered that the downfall of the family of Columbus had arrived, and some thought the Admiral would lose his head.

The news of the arrival and of the insolent conduct of Aguado reached Columbus in the interior of the island, and he immediately hastened to Isabella to meet him. As every one knew the lofty spirit of Columbus, his high sense of his services, and his jealous maintenance of his official dignity, a violent explosion was anticipated at the impending interview. The natural heat and impetuosity of Columbus, however, had been subdued by a life of trials, and he had learnt to bring his passions into subjection to his judgment; he had too true an estimate of his own dignity to enter into a contest with a shallow boaster like Aguado: above all, he had a profound reverence for the authority of his sovereigns; for, in his enthusiastic spirit, prone to deep feelings of reverence, loyalty was inferior only to religion. He received Aguado, therefore with the most grave and punctilious courtesy, ordered his letter of credence to be again proclaimed by sound of trumpet, and assured him of his readiness to agree to whatever might be the pleasure of his sovereigns.

The moderation of Columbus was regarded by many, and by Aguado himself, as a proof of his loss of moral courage. Every dastard spirit who had any lurking ill will, any real or imaginary cause of complaint, now hastened to give it utterance. It was a time of jubilee for offenders; every culprit started up into an accuser; every one who by negligence or crime had incurred the wholesome penalties of the laws was loud in his clamours of oppression; and all the ills of the colony, however produced, were ascribed to the mal-administration of the Admiral.

Aguado listened to every accusation with ready credulity, and having collected information sufficient, as he thought, to ensure the ruin of the Admiral and his brothers, prepared to return to Spain. Columbus resolved to do the same; for he felt that it was time to appear at court, to vindicate his conduct from the misrepresentations of his enemies and to explain the causes of the distresses of the colony, and of the disappointments with respect to revenue, which he feared might discourage the prosecution of his discoveries.

When the ships were ready to depart, a terrible storm swept the island; it was one of those awful whirlwinds which occasionally rage within the tropics, and which were called *Uricans*[1] by the Indians, a name which they still retain. Three of the ships at anchor in the harbour were sunk by it, with all who were on board; others were dashed against each other, and driven mere wrecks upon the shore. The Indians were overwhelmed with astonishment and dismay, for never in their memory, or in the traditions of their ancestors, had they known so tremendous a storm. They believed that the Deity had sent it in punishment of the cruelties and crimes of the white men, and declared that this people moved the very air, the water, and the earth to disturb their tranquil life, and to desolate their island.

The departure of Columbus, and of Aguado, was delayed until one of the shattered vessels, the *Niña*, could be repaired, and another constructed out of the fragments of the wrecks. In the meantime, information was received of rich mines in the interior of the island. A young Arragonian, named Miguel Diaz, in the sevice of the Adelantado, having wounded a companion in a quarrel, fled from the settlement, accompanied by five or six comrades, who had either been engaged in the affray, or were personally attached to him. Wandering about the island, they at length came to an Indian village, on the banks of the Ozema, where the city of San Domingo is at present situated; they were received with kindness by the natives, and resided for some time among them. The village was governed by a

[1] Hurricanes.

female cacique, who soon conceived a strong affection for the young Arragonian. A connection was formed between them, and they lived for some time very happily together. At length the remembrance of his country and his friends began to haunt the mind of the Spaniard; he longed to return to the settlement, but he dreaded the austere justice of the Adelantado. His Indian bride, observing him frequently lost in gloomy thought, drew from him the cause of his melancholy. Fearful that he would abandon her, and knowing the influence of gold over the white men, she informed him of certain rich mines in the neighbourhood, and urged him to persuade his countrymen to abandon Isabella, and remove to that part of the island, to the fertile banks of the Ozema, promising that they should be hospitably received by her nation.

Diaz was rejoiced at this intelligence, and hastened with it to the settlement, flattering himself that it would make his peace with the Adelantado. He was not mistaken. No tidings could have come more opportunely, for, if true, they would furnish the Admiral with the most effectual means of silencing the cavils of his enemies.

The Adelantado immediately set out in company with Diaz and his Indian guides. He was conducted to the banks of a river called the Hayna, where he found gold in greater quantities and larger particles than even in the rich province of Cibao, and observed several excavations, where it appeared as if mines had been worked in ancient times. Columbus was overjoyed at the sight of these specimens, brought back by the Adelantado, and was surprised to hear of the excavations, as the Indians possessed no knowledge of mining, and merely picked up the gold from the surface of the soil or the beds of the rivers. The circumstance gave rise to one of his usual veins of visionary speculation. He had already surmised that Hispaniola might be the ancient Ophir; he now fancied he had discovered the identical mines from whence King Solomon had procured his great supplies of gold for the building of the temple of Jerusalem. He gave orders that a fortress should be immediately erected in the vicinity of the mines, and that they should be diligently worked; and he now looked forward with confidence to his return to Spain, the bearer of such golden tidings.

It may not be uninteresting to mention that Miguel Diaz remained faithful to his Indian bride, who was baptised by the name of Catalina.

THIRD VOYAGE, 1498

CHAPTER IX

RETURN OF COLUMBUS TO SPAIN—RECEPTION BY THE SOVEREIGNS—PREPARATIONS FOR A THIRD VOYAGE.

THE new caravel, the *Santa Cruz*, being finished, and the *Niña* repaired, Columbus gave the command of the island during his absence to his brother, Don Bartholomew. He then embarked on board of one of the caravels, and Aguado in the other. The vessels were crowded with two hundred and twenty-five passengers, the sick, the idle, the profligate and factious of the colony. Never did a more miserable and disappointed crew return from a land of promise. There were thirty Indians also on board.

The Admiral had promised to restore them to their country and their power, after having presented them to the sovereigns; trusting, by kind treatment and a display of the wonders of Spain, to conquer their hostility, and convert them into important instruments for the quiet subjection of the island.

Being as yet but little experienced in the navigation of these seas, Columbus, instead of working up to the northward, so as to fall in with the tract of westerly winds, took an easterly course on leaving the island. His voyage, in consequence, became a toilsome and tedious struggle against the trade winds and calms which prevail between the tropics. Though he sailed on the 10th of March, yet on the 6th of April he was still in the vicinity of the Caribbean Islands, and had to touch at Guadaloupe to procure provisions. Here skirmishes occurred with the fierce natives. Several were taken prisoner; they were naked, and wore their hair loose and flow-

APRIL

ing upon their shoulders, though some decorated their heads with tufts of feathers. Their weapons were bows and arrows. Among them was the wife of a cacique, a woman of a proud and resolute spirit. On the approach of the Spaniards she had fled with an agility that soon distanced all pursuers, excepting a native of the Canary Islands, noted for swiftness of foot. She would have escaped even from him, but perceiving that he was alone, and far from his companions, she suddenly turned upon him, seized him by the throat, and would have strangled him, had not the Spaniards arrived and taken her, entangled like a hawk with her prey.

Columbus left Guadaloupe on the 20th of April, still working his way against the whole current of the trade winds. MAY By the 20th of May but a portion of the voyage was performed, yet the provisions were so much exhausted that every one was put on an allowance of six ounces of bread, and a pint and a half of water. By the beginning of June JUNE there was an absolute famine on board the ships, and some proposed that they should kill and eat their Indian prisoners, or throw them into the sea as so many useless mouths. Nothing but the absolute authority of Columbus prevented this last counsel from being adopted. He represented that the Indians were their fellow-beings, some of them Christians like themselves, and all entitled to similar treatment. He exhorted them to a little patience, assuring them they would soon make land, as, according to his reckoning, they could not be far from Cape St. Vincent. They scoffed at his words, for they believed themselves as yet far from their desired haven. The next morning, however, proved the correctness of his calculations, for they made the very land he had predicted.

On the 11th of June the vessels anchored in the Bay of Cadiz. The populace crowded to witness the landing of the gay and bold adventurers, who had sailed from this very port animated by the most sanguine expectations. Instead, however, of a joyous crew, bounding on shore, flushed with success, and rich with the spoils of the golden Indies, a feeble train of wretched men crawled forth, emaciated by the diseases of the colony and the hardships of the voyage; who carried in their yellow countenances, says an old writer[1], a mockery of that gold which had been the object of their search; and who had nothing to relate of the New World but tales of sickness, poverty, and disappointment.

The appearance of Columbus himself was a kind of comment on his fortunes. Either considering himself in disgrace with the sovereigns, or having made some penitential vow, he was clad in the habit of a Franciscan monk, girded with a cord, and he had suffered his beard to grow like the friars of that order. But however humble he might be in his own personal appearance, he endeavoured to keep alive the public interest in his discoveries. On his way to Burgos, to meet the sovereigns, he made a studious display of the coronets, collars, bracelets, and other ornaments of gold which he had brought from the New World. He carried with him, also, several Indians, decorated with glittering ornaments.

The reception of Columbus by the sovereigns was different from what he had anticipated, for he was treated with distinguished favour; nor was any mention made either of the complaints of Margarite and Boyle, or the judicial inquiries conducted by Aguado. However these may have had a transient effect upon the minds of the sovereigns, they were too conscious of his great deserts, and of the extraordinary difficulties of his situation, not to tolerate what they may have considered errors on his part.

Encouraged by the interest with which the sovereigns listened to his account of his recent voyage along the coast of Cuba, bordering, as he supposed, on the rich territories of the Grand Khan, and of his discovery of the mines at Hayna, which he represented as the Ophir of the ancients, Columbus now proposed a further enterprise, by which he promised to make yet more extensive discoveries, and to annex a vast and unappropriated portion of the continent of Asia to their dominions. All he asked was eight ships, two to be dispatched to Hispaniola with supplies, the remaining six to be put under his command for the voyage.

[1] La Casas.

The sovereigns readily promised to comply with his request, and were probably sincere in their intentions to do so; but in the performance of their promise Columbus was doomed to meet with intolerable delay. The resources of Spain at this moment were taxed to the utmost by the ambition of Ferdinand, who lavished all revenues in war-like enterprises. While maintaining a contest of deep and artful policy with France, with the ultimate aim of grasping the sceptre of Naples, he was laying the foundation of a wide and powerful connection by the marriages of the royal children, who were now maturing in years. At this time rose that family alliance which afterwards consolidated such an immense empire under his grandson and successor, Charles the Fifth.

These widely extended operations of war put all the land and naval forces into requisition, drained the royal treasury, and engrossed the time and thoughts of the sovereigns. It was not until the spring of 1497 that Isabella could find leisure to enter fully into the concerns of the New World. She then took them up with a spirit that showed she was determined to place them upon a substantial foundation, as well as clearly to define the powers and reward the services of Columbus. To her protecting zeal all the provisions in favour of the latter must be attributed, for the King began to look coldly on him, and Fonseca, who had most influence in the affairs of the Indies, was his implacable enemy.

As the expenses of the expeditions had hitherto exceeded the returns, Columbus was relieved of his eighth part of the cost of the past enterprises and allowed an eighth part of the gross proceeds for the next three years, and a tenth of the net profits. He was allowed also to establish a Mayorazgo, or entailed estate, in his family, of which he immediately availed himself, dividing his estates to his male descendants, with the express charge that this successor should never use any other title in signature than simply *The Admiral*. As he had felt aggrieved by the royal license for general discovery, granted in 1495, it was annulled as far as it might be prejudicial to his interests, or to the previous grants made him by the Crown. The titles and prerogatives of Adelantado were likewise conferred upon Don Bartholomew, though the King had at first been displeased with Columbus for investing his brother with dignities which were only in the gift of the sovereign.

While all these measures were taken for the immediate gratification of Columbus, others were adopted for the good of the colony. The precise number of persons was fixed who were to be sent to Hispaniola, among whom were several females; and regulations were made for their payment and support, and for the distribution of lands among them, to be diligently cultivated. The greatest care was enjoined likewise by Isabella in the religious instruction of the natives, and the utmost lenity in collecting the tributes imposed upon them. With respect to the government of the colony also, it was generally recommended that, whenever the public safety did not require stern measures, there should be manifested a disposition to indulgent and easy rule.

When every intention was thus shown on the part of the Crown to dispatch the expedition, unexpected difficulties arose on the part of the public. The charm was dispelled which, in the preceding voyage, had made every adventurer crowd into the service of Columbus; the new-found world, instead of a region of wealth and enjoyment, was now considered a land of poverty and disaster. To supply the want of voluntary recruits, therefore, Columbus proposed to transport to Hispaniola, for a limited term of years, all criminals condemned to banishment or the galleys, excepting such as had committed crimes of an atrocious nature. This pernicious measure shows the desperate alternative to which he was reduced by the reaction of public sentiment. It proved a fruitful source of misery and disaster to the colony; and having frequently been adopted by various nations, whose superior experience should have taught them better, has proved the bane of many a rising settlement.

Notwithstanding all these expedients, and the urgent representations of Columbus of the sufferings to which the colony must be reduced for want of supplies, it was not until the beginning of 1498 that the two ships were dispatched to Hispaniola, under the command of Pedro Fernandez Coronal. A still further delay occurred in fitting out the six ships that were to bear Columbus on his voyage of discovery. His cold-blooded enemy Fonseca, who was now Bishop of Badajoz, having the superintendence of Indian affairs, was enabled to impede and retard all his plans. The various officers and agents employed in the concerns of the armament were most of them dependents of the bishop, and sought to gratify him by throwing all kinds of difficulties in the way of Columbus, treating him with that arrogance which petty and ignoble men are prone to exercise, when they think they can do so with impunity. So wearied and disheartened did he become by these delays, and by the prejudices of the fickle public, that he at one time thought of abandoning his discoveries altogether.

JANUARY

The insolence of these worthless men harassed him to the last moment of his sojourn in Spain, and followed him to the water's edge. One of the most noisy and presuming was one Ximeno de Breviesca, treasurer of Fonseca, a converted Jew or Moor, and a man of impudent front and unbridled tongue, who, echoing the sentiment of his patron the bishop, had been loud in his abuse of the Admiral and his enterprises.

At the very time that Columbus was on the point of embarking, he was assailed by the insolence of Ximeno. Forgetting in the hurry and indignation of the moment, his usual self-command, he struck the despicable treasurer to the earth, and spurned him with his foot, venting in this unguarded paroxysm the accumulated griefs and vexations which had long rankled in his heart. This transport of passion, so unusual in his well-governed temper, was artfully made use of by Fonseca and others of his enemies, to injure him in the royal favour. The personal castigation of a public officer was represented as a flagrant instance of his vindictive temper, and a corroboration of the charges of cruelty and oppression sent home from the colony; and we are assured that certain humiliating measures, shortly afterwards adopted towards him, were in consequence of the effect produced upon the sovereigns by these false accounts.

Columbus himself deeply regretted his indiscretion, and foresaw the invidious use that would be made of it. It would be difficult to make, with equal brevity, a more direct and affecting appeal than that contained in one of his letters, wherein he alludes to this affair. He entreats the sovereigns not to let it be wrested to his injury in their opinion; but to remember, when anything should be said to his disparagement, that he was "absent, envied, and a stranger".

CHAPTER X

EVENTS DURING THE VOYAGE—DISCOVERY OF TRINIDAD —ADMINISTRATION OF HAITI BY BARTHOLOMEW— CONSPIRACY AND REBELLION OF ROLDAN—COLUMBUS MEETS BARTHOLOMEW AT SAN DOMINGO.

ON the 30th of May, 1498, Columbus set sail from the port of San Lucar de Barrameda, with a squadron of six vessels, on his third voyage of discovery. From various considerations, he was induced to take a different route from that pursued in his former expeditions. He had been assured, by persons who had traded to the East, that the rarest objects of commerce, such as gold, precious stones, drugs, and spices, were chiefly to be found in the regions about the equator, where the inhabitants were black or darkly coloured; and that, until he arrived among people of such complexions, it was not probable he would find those articles in great abundance.

MAY

Columbus expected to find such people more to the south and southeast. He recollected that the natives of Hispaniola had spoken of black men who had once come to their island from the south, the heads of whose javelins were of guanin, or adulterated gold. The natives of the Caribbean Islands, also, had informed him that a great tract of the mainland lay to the south; and in his preceding voyage he had remarked that Cuba, which he supposed to be the continent of Asia, swept off in that direction.

He proposed, therefore, to take his departure from the Cape de Verde Islands, sailing to the southwest until he should come under the equinoctial line, then to steer directly westward, with the favour of the trade winds.

Having touched at the islands of Porto Santo and Madeira,

to take in wood and water, he continued his course to the Canary Islands, from whence he dispatched three of his ships direct for Hispaniola, with supplies for the colony. With the remaining three he prosecuted his voyage towards the Cape de Verde Islands. The ship in which he sailed was decked, the other two were merchant caravels. As he advanced within the tropics, the change of climate and the close and sultry weather brought on a severe attack of the gout, accompanied by a violent fever; but he still enjoyed the full possession of his faculties, and continued to keep his reckoning and make his observations with his usual vigilance and minuteness.

On the 5th of June he took his departure from the Cape de Verde Islands, and steered to the southwest until he arrived, according to his observations, in the fifth degree of north latitude[1]. Here the wind suddenly fell, and a dead, sultry calm succeeded. The air was like a furnace, the tar melted from the sides of the ships, the seams yawned, the salt meat became putrid, the wheat was parched as if with fire, some of the wine and water casks burst, and the heat in the holds of the vessels was so suffocating that no one could remain below to prevent the damage that was taking place among the sea stores. The mariners lost all strength and spirits. It seemed as if the old fable of the torrid zone was about to be realised, and that they were approaching a fiery region where it would be impossible to exist. It is true, the heavens became overcast, and there were drizzling showers, but the atmosphere was close and stifling, and there was that combination of heat and moisture which relaxes all the energies of the human frame.

JUNE

A continuation of this weather, together with the remonstrances of his crew, and his extreme suffering from the gout, ultimately induced him to alter his route, and stand to the northwest, in hopes of falling in with the Caribbean Islands, where he might repair his ships, and obtain water and provisions. After sailing some distance in this direction, through an ordeal of heats and calms, and murky, stifling atmosphere, the ships all at once emerged into a genial region; a pleasant, cool-

[1] 5° North of the Equator.

ing breeze played over the sea, and gently filled their sails; the sky became serene and clear, and the sun shone forth with all its splendour, but no longer with a burning heat.

On the 31st of July, when there was not above a cask of water remaining in each ship, a mariner, named Alonzo Perez, descried, from the masthead, three mountains rising above the horizon. As the ships drew nearer, these mountains proved to be united at the base. Columbus, therefore, from a religious association of ideas, gave this island the name of La Trinidad[1], which it continues to bear at the present day.

AUGUST

Shaping his course for this island, he approached its eastern extremity, to which he gave the name of Punta de Galera, from a rock in the sea which resembled a galley under sail. He then coasted along the southern shore, between Trinidad and the mainland, which he beheld on the south, stretching to the distance of more than twenty leagues. It was that low tract of coast intersected by the numerous branches of the Orinoco, but the Admiral, supposing it to be an island, gave it the name of La Isla Santa; little imagining that he now, for the first time, beheld that continent, that *terra firma*, which had been the object of his earnest searchings.

He was for several days coasting the island of Trinidad, and exploring the great Gulf of Paria, which lies behind it, fancying himself among islands, and that he must find a passage to the open ocean by keeping to the bottom of the gulf. During this time he was nearly swept from his anchors and thrown on shore by a sudden rush and swell of the sea, near Point Arenal, between Trinidad and the mainland, caused, it is supposed, by the swelling of one of the rivers which flow into the gulf. He landed on the inside of the long promontory of Paria, which he mistook for an island, and had various interviews with the natives, from whom he procured great quantities of pearls, many of a fine size and quality.

There were several phenomena that surprised and perplexed Columbus in the course of his voyage along this coast, and

[1] La Trinadad, the Trinity.

which gave rise to speculations, some ingenious and others fanciful. He was astonished at the vast body of fresh water continually flowing into the gulf of Paria, so as apparently to sweeten the whole surrounding sea, and at the constant current which set through it, which he supposed to be produced by some great river. He remarked, with wondering, also, the difference between the climate, vegetation, and people of these coasts, and those of the same parallel in Africa. There the heat was insupportable and the land parched and sterile, the inhabitants were black, with crisped wool, ill-shapen, and of dull and brutal natures.

Here, on the contrary, although the sun was in Leo, he found the noontide heat moderate, the mornings and evenings fresh and cool, the country green and fruitful, covered with beautiful forests and watered by innumerable streams and fountains; the people fairer than even those in the lands he had discovered further north, with long hair, well proportioned and graceful forms, lively minds, and courageous spirits. In respect to the vast body of fresh water, he made one of his simple and great conclusions. Such a mighty stream could not be produced by an island; it must be the outpouring of a continent. He now supposed that the various tracts of land which he had beheld about the gulf were connected together, and continued to an immense distance to the south, far beyond the equator, into that hemisphere hitherto unknown to civilised man.

As to the mild temperature of the climate, the fresh verdure of the country, and the comparative fairness of the inhabitants, in a parallel so near to the equator, he attributed it to the superior elevation of this part of the globe; for, from a variety of circumstances, ingeniously but erroneously reasoned upon, he inferred that philosophers had been mistaken in the form of the earth, which, instead of being a perfect sphere, he now concluded to be shaped like a pear, one part more elevated than the rest, rising into the purer regions of the air, above the heats and frosts and storms of the lower parts of the earth. He imagined this apex to be situated about the equinoctial line, in the interior of this vast continent, which he considered the extremity of the East; that on this summit, as it were, of the earth was situated the terrestrial paradise; and that the vast stream of fresh water which poured into the Gulf of Paria issued from the fountain of the tree of life, in the midst of the Garden of Eden. Extravagant as this speculation may seem at the present day, it was grounded on the writings of the most sage and learned men of those times, among whom the situation of the terrestrial paradise had long been a subject of discussion and controversy, and by several of whom it was supposed to be on a vast mountain, in the remote parts of the East.

The mind of Columbus was so possessed by these theories, and he was so encouraged by the quantities of pearls which he had found for the first time in the New World, that he would gladly have followed up his discovery, not doubting but that the country would increase in the value of its productions as he approached the equator. The sea stores of his ships, however, were almost exhausted, and the various supplies with which they were freighted for the colony were in danger of spoiling. He was suffering, also, extremely in his health. Besides the gout, which had rendered him a cripple for the greater part of the voyage, he was afflicted by a complaint in his eyes, caused by fatigue and over-watching, which almost deprived him of sight. He determined, therefore, to hasten to Hispaniola, intending to repose there from his fatigues, and recruit his health, while he should send his brother, the Adelantado, to complete this important discovery.

On the 11th of August, therefore, he left the gulf, by a narrow strait between the promontory of Paria and the Island of Trinidad. This strait is beset with small islands, and the current which sets through the gulf is so compressed between them as to cause a turbulent sea, with great foaming and roaring, as if rushing over rocks and shoals. The Admiral conceived himself in imminent danger of shipwreck when passing through this strait, and gave it the name of *La Boca del Drago*, or the Mouth of the Dragon. After reconnoitring the coast to the westward, as far as the islands of Cubaga and Margarita, and convincing himself of its being a continent, he bore away for

Hispaniola, for the river Ozema, where he expected to find a new settlement, which he had instructed his brother to form in the neighbourhood of the mines. He was borne far to the westward by the currents, but at length reached his desired haven, where he arrived, haggard, emaciated, and almost blind, and was received with open arms by the Adelantado. The brothers were strongly attached to each other; Don Bartholomew had a great deference of the brilliant genius, and the commanding reputation of his brother; while the latter placed great reliance, in times of difficulty, on the worldly knowledge, the indefatigable activity, and the lion-hearted courage of the Adelantado. They had both, during their long separation, experienced the need of each other's sympathy and support.

Columbus had anticipated a temporary repose from his toils on arriving at Hispaniola; but a new scene of trouble and anxiety opened upon him, which was destined to affect all his future fortunes. To explain this, it is necessary to state the occurrences of the island during his long detention in Spain.

When he sailed for Europe in March, 1496, his brother, Don Bartholomew, immediately proceeded to execute his instructions with respect to the gold mines of Hayna. He built a fortress in the neighbourhood, which he named San Christoval, and another fortress not far off, on the eastern bank of the Ozema, in the vicinity of the village inhabited by the female cacique who had first given intelligence of the mines to Miguel Diaz. This fortress was called San Domingo, and was the origin of the city which still bears that name.

Having garrisoned these fortresses, and made arrangements for working the mines, the indefatigable Adelantado set out to visit the dominions of Behechio, which had not as yet been reduced to obedience. This cacique, as has been mentioned, reigned over Xaragua, a province comprising almost the whole of the west end of the island, including Cape Tiburon. It was one of the most populous and fertile districts. The inhabitants were finely formed, had a noble air, a more agreeable elocution, and more soft and graceful manners than the natives of the other part of the island. The Indians of Haiti generally placed their elysium, or paradise of happy spirits, in the delightful valleys that bordered the great lake of Xaragua.

Don Bartholomew entered the province of Xaragua at the head of an armed band, putting his cavalry in the advance, and marching with banners displayed, and the sound of drum and trumpet. Behechio met him with a numerous force, but being assured that he came merely on a friendly visit, he dismissed his army, and conducted the Adelantado to his residence in a large town, near the deep bay called at present the Bight of Leagon.

As they approached, thirty young females of the cacique's household came forth to meet them, waving palm branches, and dancing, and singing their areytos or traditionary ballads. When they came before Don Bartholomew they knelt and laid their palm branches at his feet. After these came the beautiful Anacaona, sister of Behechio, reclining on a litter, borne by six Indians. She was lightly clad in a robe of various coloured cotton, with a fragrant garland of red and white flowers round her head, and wreaths of the same round her neck and arms. She received the Adelantado with a natural grace and courtesy.

For several days Don Bartholomew remained in Xaragua, entertained by the cacique and his sister with banquets, national games and dances, and other festivities; then, having arranged for a periodical tribute to be paid in cotton, hemp, and cassava bread, the productions of the surrounding country, he took a friendly leave of his hospitable entertainers, and set out with his little army for Isabella.

He found the settlement in a sickly state, and suffering from a scarcity of provisions; he distributed, therefore, all that were too feeble to labour or bear arms, into the interior, where they might have better air and more abundant food; and at the same time he established a chain of fortresses between Isabella and San Domingo. Insurrections broke out among the natives of the vega, caused by their impatience of tribute, by the outrages of some of the Spaniards, and by a severe punishment inflicted on certain Indians for the alleged violation of a Chapel. Guarionex, a man naturally moderate and peaceful, was persuaded by his brother caciques to take up arms, and a combination was formed among them to rise suddenly upon the Spaniards, massacre them, and destroy Fort Conception, which was situated in the vega. By some means the garrison received intimation of the conspiracy. They immediately wrote a letter to the Adelantado, imploring prompt assistance. How to convey the letter in safety was an anxious question, for the natives had discovered that these letters had a wonderful power of communicating intelligence, and fancied that they could talk. An Indian undertook to be the bearer of it. He enclosed it in a staff, and set out on his journey. Being intercepted, he pretended to be dumb and lame, leaning upon his staff for support. He was allowed to depart, and limped forward until out of sight, when he resumed his speed, and bore the letter safely and expeditiously to San Domingo.

The Adelantado, with his accustomed promptness, set out with a body of troops for the fortress. By a rapid and well-concerted stratagem he surprised the leaders in the night, in a village in which they were sleeping, and carried them all off captive, seizing upon Guarionex with his own hand. He completed his enterprise with spirit, sagacity, and moderation. Informing himself of the particulars of the conspiracy, he punished two caciques, the principal movers of it, with death, and pardoned all the rest. Finding, moreover, that Guarionex had been chiefly incited to hostility by an outrage committed by a Spaniard on his wife, he inflicted punishment on the offender. The heart of Guarionex was subdued by the unexpected clemency of the Adelantado, and he made a speech to his subjects in praise of the Spaniards. They listened to him with attention, and when he had concluded, bore him off on their shoulders with songs and shouts of joy, and for some time the tranquillity of the vega was restored.

About this time, receiving information from Behechio, cacique of Xaragua, that his tribute in cotton and provisions was ready for delivery, the Adelantado marched there, at the head of his forces, to receive it. So large a quantity of cotton and cassava bread was collected together that Don Bartholomew

THE SPANISH LETTER OF COLUMBUS TO LUIS DE SANT' ANGEL

Dated 15th February, 1493

Sir,

As I know that you will have pleasure of the great victory which our Lord hath given me in my voyage, I write you this, by which you shall know that, in [thirty-three] days I passed over to the Indies with the fleet which the most illustrious King and Queen, our Lords, gave me: where I found very many islands peopled with inhabitants beyond number. And, of them all, I have taken possession for their Highnesses, with proclamation and the royal standard displayed; and I was not gainsaid. On the first which I found, I put the name Sant Salvador, in commemoration of His high Majesty, who marvellously hath [given] all this: the Indians call it [Guanaham][1]. The second I named the Island of Santa Maria de Concepcion, the third Ferrandina, the fourth, [Fair Island][2], the fifth La Isla Juana; and so for each one a new name. When I reached Juana, I followed its coast westwardly, and found it so large that I thought it might be the mainland province of Cathay. And as I did not thus find any towns and villages on the sea-coast, save small hamlets with the people whereof I could not get speech, because they all fled away forthwith, I went on further in the same direction, thinking I should not miss of great cities or towns. And at the end of many leagues, seeing that there was no change, and that the coast was bearing me northwards, whereunto my desire was contrary since the winter was already confronting us, I formed the purpose of making from thence to the south, and as the wind also blew against me, I determined not to wait for other weather and turned back as far as a port agreed upon; from which I sent two men into the country to learn if there were a King, or any great cities. They travelled for three days, and found innumerable small villages and a numberless population, but nought of ruling authority; wherefore they returned. . .

[1] Guanahani
[2] Isabella

* * *

The above is a literal translation of part of this letter. It was sent by Columbus from the Canary Islands, and was four pages in length. A facsimile of page one is reproduced facing this page.

SEÑOR porque se que aureis plazer dela grand vitoria que nuestro señor me
ha dado en mi viaie vos escrivo esta por la q̃l sabreys como en veinte dias pase A
las idias cō la armada q̄ los illustrissimos Rey e Reyna ñros señores me dieron
dōde yo falle muy muchas Yslas pobladas cō gente sin numero: y dellas todas
he tomado posesion por sus altezas con pregon y vādera real estendida y non me fue
cōtradicho. Ala primera q̄ yo falle puse nonbre sant saluador a comemoracion de su alta mages
tat el qual maravillosamente todo esto anodado los idios la llaman guanahani. Ala segūda
puse nonbre la isla de santa maria deconcepcion ala tercera ferrandina ala quarta la isla bella
ala quīta la Ysla Juana e asi a cada vna nonbre nuevo. Quando yo llegue ala Juana seg
ui io la costa della al poniente y la falle tan grande q̄ pense que seria tierra firme la provīcia de
catayo y como no falle asi villas y luguares ēla costa dela mar saluo pequeñas poblaciones
con lagente delas q̃ules nopodia haver fabla porque luego fuyan todos: andaua yo a de
lante por el dicho camino pēsādo deno errar grādes Ciudades o villas y al cabo de muchas
leguas visto q̄ no havia inovaciō i que la costa me levava alsetētrion de adōde mi voluntad
era cōtraria porq̄ el yvierno era ya ēcarnado yo tenia proposito de hazer del al austro y tanbiē
el viēto me dio adelāte determine deno aguardar otro tiēpo y bolui atras fasta vn señalado puer
to de adōde ēbie dos hōbres por la tierra para saber si havia Rey o grādes Ciudades. ādovi
erō tres iornadas y hallarō īfinitas poblaciōes pequeñas i gēte sī numero mas no cosa de reg
imiēto por lo qual se bolvierō yo entēdia harto de otros idios q̄ ia tenia tomados como conti
nuamēte esta tierra era Ysla e asi segui la costa della al oriēte ciento i siete leguas fasta dōde fa
zia fin: del qual cabo vi otra Ysla al oriēte distīcta de esta diez o ocho leguas ala qual luego
puse nombre la spañola y fui alli y segui la parte del setentrion asi como dela iuana al oriente.
clxxviii grādes leguas por linia recta del oriēte asi como dela iuana la qual y todas las otras
sō fortissimas en demasiado grado y esta enestremo en ella ay muchos puertos enla costa dela
mar sī cōparaciō de otros q̄ yo sepa en cristianos y fartos rrios y buenos y grandes q̄ es mara
villa las tierras della sō altas y ē ella muy muchas sierras y mōtañas altissimas sī cōparaciō
de la isla de cētre frei todas fermosissimas de mil fechuras y todas ādabiles y llenas de arboles
de mil maneras i altas i parecen q̄ llegā al cielo i tēgo por dicho q̄ iamas pierdē la foia segun lo
puede cōprehēder q̄ los vi tā verdes i tā hermosos como sō por mayo en spaña i dellos stavā flor
ridos dellos cō fruto i dellos enotro termino segū es su calidad i cātava el ruiseñor i otros pa
xaricos de mil maneras en el mes de noviēbre por alli dōde io āndava ay palmas de seis o de
ocho maneras q̄ es admiracion verlas por la diformidad fermosa dellas mas asi como los
otros arboles y frutos eiervas en ella ay pinares a maravilla e ay canpiñas grādissimas e ay mi
el i de muchas maneras de aves y frutas muy diversas enlas tierras ay muchas minas deme
tales e ay gēte īstimabile numero. La spañola es maravilla la sierras y las mōtañas y las vegas
i las campiñas y las tierras tan fermosas y gruesas para plantar y sebrar pacer ganados de to
das suertes para hedificios de villas elugares los puertos dela mar aqui no havria chrencia sin
vista y delos rios muchos y grandes y buenas aguas los mas delos quales traē oro ē los arbo
les y frutos e yervas ay grandes differencias de aquellas dela iuana en esta ay muchas specie
rias y grandes minas de oro y de otros metales. La gente desta ysla y de todas las otras q̄ he
fallado y havido: ni aya havido noticia andan todos desnudos hōbres y mugeres asi como
sus madres los paren haun que algunas mugeres se cobiian vn solo lugar cō vna foia de yer
va: o vna cosa de algodō que pa ello fazen ellos no tienen fierro ni azero ni armas ni son
a ello no porque no sea gente bien dispuesta y de fermosa estatura saluo que sō muy te[...]
a maravilla no tienē otras armas saluo las [...]as delas cañas quando [...] cōla simiente
a la qual ponen al cabo vn palillo aguido e no [...]an vsar de aquellas que [...] veses me
acaeçio enbiar aterra dos o tres hombres [...] alguna villa pa haver fabl[...] salir a [...]

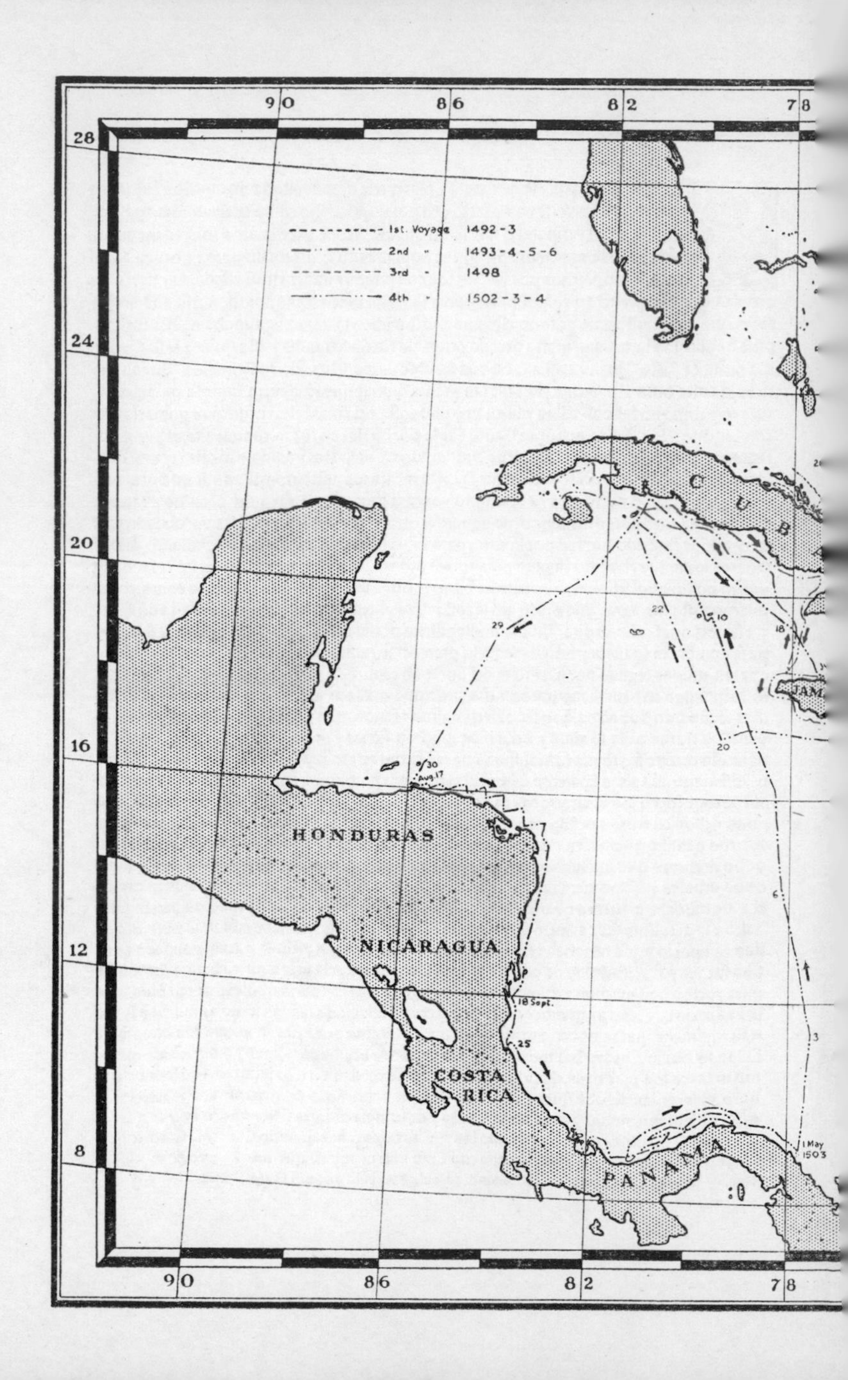

1st. Voyage 1492-3
2nd 1493-4-5-6
3rd 1498
4th 1502-3-4
HONDURAS
NICARAGUA
COSTA RICA
PANAMA
C U B
Aug. 17
18 Sept.
1 May 1503

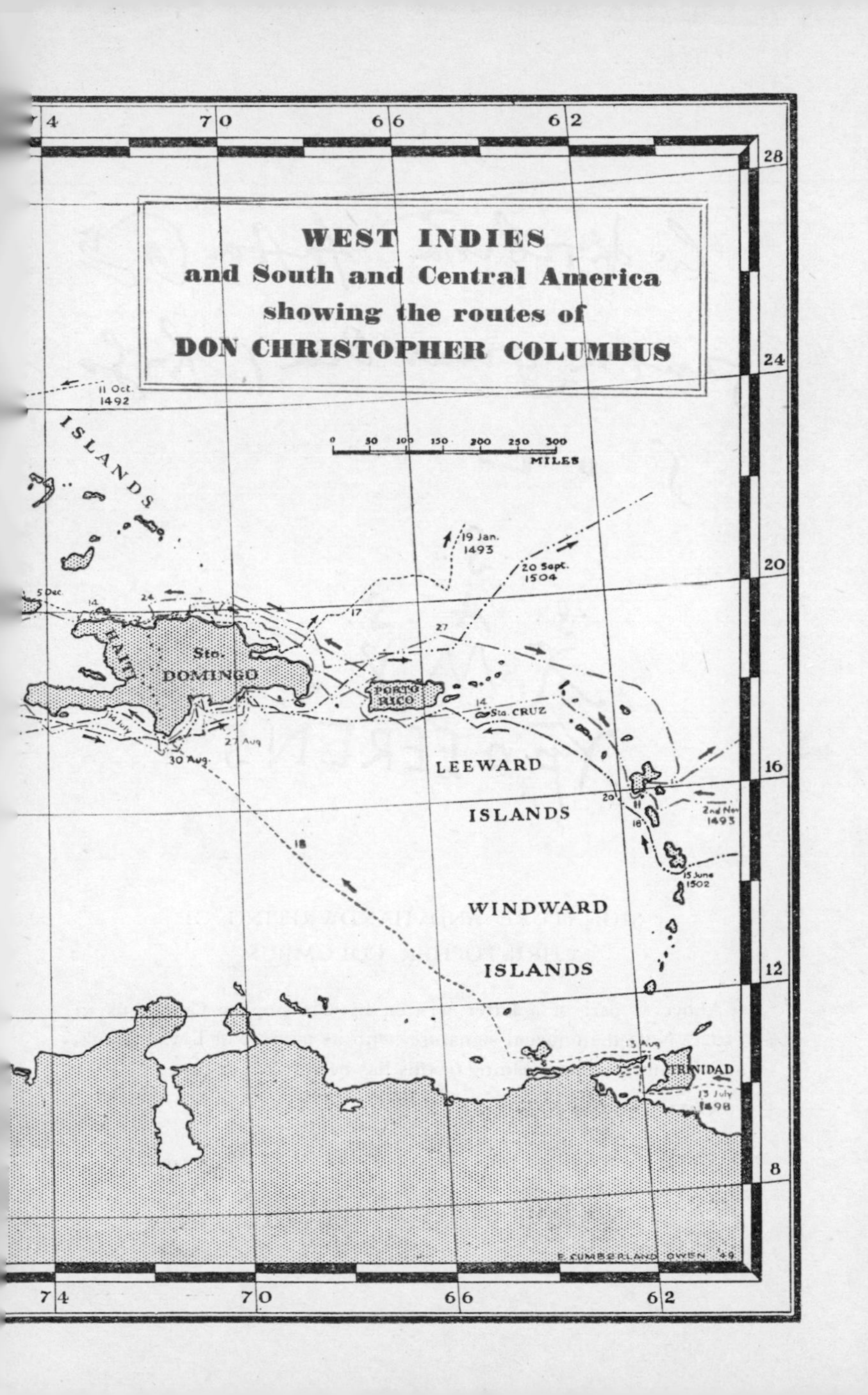
WEST INDIES
and South and Central America
showing the routes of
DON CHRISTOPHER COLUMBUS
74
70
66
62
28
24
20
16
12
8
0 50 100 150 200 250 300
MILES
11 Oct. 1492
ISLANDS
19 Jan. 1493
20 Sept. 1504
5 Dec.
14
24
17
27
HAITI
Sto. DOMINGO
PORTO RICO
14
Sta. CRUZ
14 July
27 Aug
30 Aug.
LEEWARD
ISLANDS
20
11
18
2nd Nov 1493
18
15 June 1502
WINDWARD
ISLANDS
13 Aug
TRINIDAD
13 July 1498
E. CUMBERLAND OWEN '49

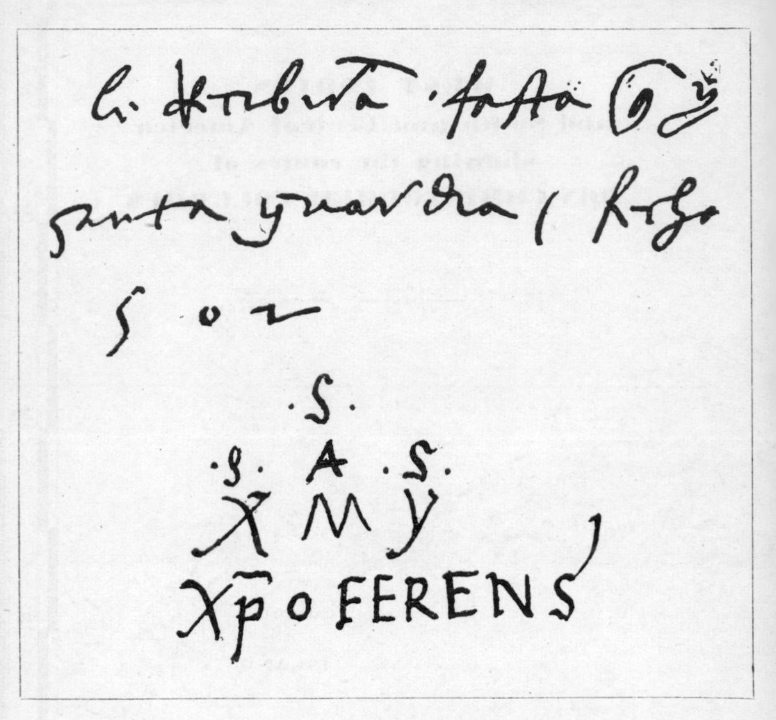

SIGNATURE AND HANDWRITING OF
CHRISTOPHER COLUMBUS

Above is part of a letter written by Christopher Columbus in 1502. Note the unusual signature, with its mixture of Latin, Greek, and Spanish. The meaning of this has been much disputed.

A likely reading is:

	.S. (alve)		Save (me)
.S.	A	.S.	
X (ristus)	M (aria)	Y (osephus)	Christ, Mary, Joseph
XpoFERENS.			Christoferens

had to send to the settlement of Isabella for a caravel to be freighted with it. In the meantime, the utmost kindness was lavished upon their guests by these gentle and generous people. The troubles which distracted the other parts of devoted Haiti had not yet reached this pleasant region; and when the Spaniards regarded the fertility and sweetness of the country, bordering on a tranquil sea, the kindness of the inhabitants, and the beauty of the women, they pronounced it a perfect paradise.

When the caravel arrived on the coast, it was regarded by Anacaona and her brother with awe and wonder. Behechio visited it with his canoes; but his sister, with her female attendants, were conveyed on board in the boat of the Adelantado. As they approached, the caravel fired a salute. At the sound of the cannon, and the sight of volumes of smoke bursting from the side of the ship and rolling along the sea, Anacaona, overcome with dismay, fell into the arms of the Adelantado, and her attendants would have leaped overboard, but were reassured by the cheerful words of Don Bartholomew. As they drew nearer the vessel several instruments of martial music struck up, with which they were greatly delighted. Their admiration increased on entering on board; but when the anchor was weighed, the sails filled by a gentle breeze, and they beheld this vast mass veering from side to side, apparently by its own will, and playing like a huge monster on the deep, the brother and sister remained gazing at each other in mute astonishment. Nothing seems ever to have filled the mind of the savage with more wonder than that beautiful triumph of human ingenuity—a ship under sail.

While the Adelantado was thus absent quelling insurrections and making skilful arrangements for the prosperity of the colony and the advantage of the Crown, new mischiefs were fermenting in the factious settlement of Isabella. The prime mover was Francisco Roldan, a man who had been raised by Columbus from poverty and obscurity, and promoted from one office to another, until he had appointed him Alcalde Mayor, or chief judge of the island. He was an uneducated man, but of strong natural talents, great assiduity, and intrepid impudence. He had seen his benefactor return to Spain apparently under a cloud of disgrace, and, considering him a fallen man, began to devise how he might profit by his downfall. He was intrusted with an office inferior only to that of the Adelantado; the brothers of Columbus were highly unpopular; he imagined it possible to ruin them, both with the colonists and with the government at home, and by dexterous management to work his way into a command of the colony. For this purpose he mingled among the common people, threw out suggestions that the Admiral was in disgrace, and would never return; railed at the Adelantado and Don Diego as foreigners, who took no interest in their welfare, but used them merely as slaves to build houses and fortresses for them, or to swell their state and secure their power, as they marched about the island, enriching themselves with the spoils of the caciques. By these seditious insinuations he exasperated their feelings to such a degree that they at one time formed a conspiracy to assassinate the Adelantado, but it was happily disconcerted, by accident.

When the caravel returned from Xaragua, laden with provisions, it was dismantled by order of Don Diego, and drawn upon the beach. Roldan immediately seized upon this circumstance to awaken new suspicions. He said the true reason for dismantling the caravel was to prevent any of the colonists returning in it to Spain, to represent the oppressions under which they suffered. He advised them to launch and take possession of the vessel, as the only means of regaining their independence. They might then throw off the tyranny of these upstart foreigners, and might lead a life of ease and quiet, employing the Indians as slaves.

Don Diego was informed of these seditious movements, but he was of a mild, pacific nature, and deficient in energy. Fearing to come to an open rupture in the mutinous state of the colony, he thought to divert Roldan from his schemes by giving him distant and active employment. He detached him suddenly, therefore, with a small force, to over-awe the Indians of the vega, who had shown a disposition to revolt. Roldan made use of this opportunity to organise an armed faction. He soon got seventy well-armed and resolute men at his command, disposed to go all desperate lengths with him, and he made friends and partisans among the discontented caciques, promising to free them from tribute. He now threw off the mask, and openly set the Adelantado and his brother at defiance, as men who had no authority from the Crown, but were appointed by Columbus, who was himself in disgrace. He pretended always to act in his official capacity, and to do everything from loyal motives, and every act of open rebellion was accompanied with shouts of "Long live the King!" Having endeavoured repeatedly to launch the caravel, but in vain, he broke open the royal stores, and supplied his followers with arms, clothing, and provisions, and then marched off to the vega, and attempted to surprise and get possession of Fort Conception, but was foiled by its commander, Miguel Ballester, an old soldier, both resolute and wary, who kept the enemy at bay until succour should arrive.

The conspiracy had attained a formidable head during the absence of the Adelantado, several persons of consequence having joined it, among whom was Adrian de Moxica and Diego de Escobar, the latter being alcalde of the fortress of La Madalena. Don Bartholomew was perplexed at first, and could not act with his usual vigour and decision, not knowing in whom he could confide, or how far the conspiracy had extended. On receiving tidings, however, from Miguel Ballester, of the danger of Fort Conception, he threw himself, with what forces he could collect, into that fortress, and held a parley with Roldan from one of the windows, ordering him to surrender his staff of office as Alcalde Mayor and submit peaceably to superior authority. All threats and remonstrances, however, were vain; Roldan persisted in his rebellion. He represented the Adelantado as the tyrant of the Spaniards, the oppressor of the Indians; and himself as the redresser of wrongs and champion of the injured. He sought, by crafty emissaries, to corrupt the garrison of Fort Conception and induce them to desert, and laid plans to surprise and seize upon the Adelantado, should he leave the fortress.

The affairs of the island were in a lamentable situation. The Indians, perceiving the dissensions among the Spaniards, and encouraged by the protection of Roldan, ceased to send in their tributes, and threw off allegiance to the government. Roldan's band daily gained strength, and ranged insolently and at large about the country; while the Spaniards who remained loyal, fearing conspiracies among the natives, had to keep under shelter of the forts. Munitions of all kinds were rapidly wasting, and the spirits of the well-affected were sinking into despondency. The Adelantado himself remained shut up in Fort Conception, doubtful of the fidelity of his own garrison, and secretly informed of the plots to capture or destroy him, should he venture abroad. Such was the desperate state to which the colony was reduced by the long detention of Columbus in Spain, and the impediments thrown in the way of all his endeavours to send out supplies and reinforcements. Fortunately, at this critical juncture the arrival of two ships, under command of Pedro Hernandez Coronal, at the port of San Domingo, with troops and provisions, strengthened the hands of Don Bartholomew. The royal confirmation of his title and authority of Adenlantado at once put an end to all question of the legitimacy of his power, and secured the fidelity of his solders; and the tidings that the Admiral was in high favour at court, and on the point of coming out with a powerful squadron, struck consternation into the rebels, who had presumed upon his having fallen into disgrace.

The Adelantado immediately hastened to San Domingo, and there was no attempt made to molest him on his march. When he found himself once more secure, his magnanimity prevailed over his indignation, and he sent Pedro Hernandez Coronal, to offer Roldan and his band amnesty for all offences, on condition of instant obedience. Roldan feared to venture into his power, and determined to prevent the emissary from communicating with his followers, lest they should be induced to return to their allegiance. When Coronal approached the encampment of the rebels, therefore, he was opposed in a narrow pass by a body of archers with their crossbows levelled. "Halt there, traitor!" cried Roldan; "had you arrived eight days later, we should all have been united."

It was in vain that Coronal endeavoured to win this turbulent man from his revolt. He professsd to oppose only the tyranny and misrule of the Adelantado, but to be ready to submit to the Admiral on his arrival, and he and his principal confederates wrote letters to that effect to their friends in San Domingo.

When Coronal returned with accounts of Roldan's contumacy, the Adelantado proclaimed him and his followers traitors. That shrewd rebel, however, did not suffer his men to remain within the reach either of promise or menace. He proposed to them to march off and establish themselves in the remote province of Xaragua. The Spaniards who had been there had given the most alluring accounts of the country and its inhabitants, and above all of the beauty of the women. In this delightful region, emancipated from the iron rule of the Adelantado, and relieved from the necessity of irksome labour, they might lead a life of perfect freedom and indulgence, with a world of beauty at their command. In short, Roldan drew a picture of carefree enjoyment, such as he knew to be irresistible with men of idle and dissolute habits. His followers acceded with joy to his proposition; so, putting himself at their head, he marched away for Xaragua.

Scarcely had the rebels departed when fresh insurrections broke out among the Indians of the vega. The cacique Guarionex, moved by the instigations of Roldan, and forgetful of his gratitude to Don Bartholomew, entered into a new league to destroy the Spaniards, and surprise Fort Conception. The plot exploded before its time, and was defeated; and Guarionex, hearing that the Adelantado was on the march for the vega, fled to the mountains of Ciguay, with his family, and a small band of faithful followers. The inhabitants of these mountains were the most robust and hardy tribe of the island, and the same who had skirmished with the Spaniards in the Gulf of Samana, in the course of the first voyage of Columbus.

The Adelantado pursued Guarionex to the mountains, at the head of ninty men, and a body of Indians. It was a rugged and difficult enterprise; the troops had to climb rocks, wade rivers, and make their way through tangled forests, almost impervious to men in armour, encumbered with targets, cross-bows, and lances. They were continually exposed, also, to the ambushes of the Indians, who would rush forth with furious yells, discharge their weapons, and then take refuge again among rocks and thickets, where it was in vain to follow them. Don Bartholomew arrived, at length, in the neighbourhood of Cape Cabron, the residence of the cacique Mayonabex, and sent a messenger, demanding the surrender of Guarionex, promising friendship in case of compliance, but threatening to lay waste his territory in case of refusal. "Tell the Spaniards", said the cacique, in reply, "that they are tyrants, usurpers, and shedders of innocent blood, and I desire not their friendship. Guarionex is a good man, and my friend. He has fled to me for refuge; I have promised him protection, and I will keep my word."

The cacique, in fact, adhered to his promise with admirable faith. His villages were burnt, his territories were ravaged, himself and his family driven to dens and caves of the mountains, and his subjects assailed him with protests, urging him to give up the fugitive, who was bringing such ruin upon their tribe. It was all in vain. He was ready, he declared, to abide all evils, rather than it should ever be said Mayonabex betrayed his guest.

For three months the Adelantado hunted these caciques among the mountains, during which time he and his soldiers were almost worn out with toil and hunger, and exposures of all kind. The retreat of Mayonabex was at length discovered. Twelve Spaniards, disguising themselves as Indians, and wrapping their swords in palm leaves, came upon him secretly, and surprised and captured him, with his wife and children and a few attendants. The Adelantado returned, with his prisoners, to Fort Conception, where he afterwards released them all, excepting the cacique, whom he detained as a hostage for the submission of his tribe. The unfortunate Guarionex still lurked among the caverns of the mountains, but was driven by hunger to venture down occasionally into the plain, in quest of food. His haunts were discovered, he was waylaid and captured by a party of Spaniards, and brought in chains to Fort Conception. After his repeated insurrections, and the extraordinary zeal displayed in his pursuit, he anticipated death from the vengeance of the Adelantado. Don Bartholomew, however, though stern in his policy, was neither vindictive nor cruel; he contented himself with detaining him a prisoner, to insure the tranquillity of the vega; and then returned to San Domingo, where, shortly afterwards, he had the happiness of welcoming the arrival of his brother, the Admiral, after a separation of nearly two years and a half.

CHAPTER XI

ROLDAN DEFIES COLUMBUS—A FURTHER MUTINY—CAPITULATION WITH ROLDAN—DEPARTURE OF REBELS FOR SPAIN—ARRIVAL OF OJEDA AT THE WESTERN PART OF THE ISLAND—CONSPIRACY OF MOXICA.

ONE of the measures of Columbus, on his arrival, was to issue a proclamation, approving of all that the Adelantado had done, and denouncing Roldan and his associates. That turbulent man had proceeded to Xaragua, where he had been kindly received by the natives. A circumstance occurred to add to his party and his resources. The three caravels detached by Columbus from the Canary Islands, and freighted with supplies, having been carried far west of their reckoning by the currents, arrived on the coast of Xaragua. The rebels were at first alarmed lest these should be vessels dispatched in pursuit of them. Roldan, who was as sagacious as he was bold, soon divined the truth. Enjoining the utmost secrecy on his men, he went on board, and pretending to be in command at that end of the island, succeeded in procuring a supply of arms and military stores, and in making partisans among the crews, many of whom were criminals and vagabonds from Spanish prisons, shipped in compliance with the Admiral's ill-judged proposition.

It was not until the third day that Alonzo Sanchez de Carvajal, the most intelligent of the three captains, discovered the real character of the guests he had entertained, but the mischief was then effected.

As the ships were detained by contrary winds, it was arranged among the captains that a large number of the people should be conducted by land to San Domingo, by Juan Antonio Colombo, captain of one of the caravels, and a relation of the

Admiral. He accordingly landed with forty men, well armed, but was astonished to find himself suddenly deserted by all his party excepting eight. The deserters joined the rebels, who received them with shouts of exultation. Juan Antonio, grieved and disconcerted, returned on board with the few who remained faithful. Fearing further desertions, the ships immediately put to sea; but Carvajal, giving his vessel in charge to his officers, landed and remained with the rebels, fancying he had seen signs of wavering in Roldan and some of his associates, and that, by earnest persuasion, he might induce them to return to their allegiance.

The certainty that Columbus was actually on the way to the island, with additional forces and augmented authority, had in fact, operated strongly on their minds; but all attempts to produce immediate submission were in vain. Roldan promised that the moment he heard of the arrival of Columbus he would repair to the neighbourhood of San Domingo, to be at hand to state his grievances, and to enter into a negotiation for the adjustment of all differences. He wrote a letter to be delivered to the Admiral. With this Carvajal departed, and was escorted to within six leagues of San Domingo, by six of the rebels. On reaching that place he found Columbus already arrived, and delivered to him the letter of Roldan, expressing at the same time an opinion that the insurgents might easily be brought to their allegiance by an assurance of amnesty. In fact, the rebels soon began to assemble at the village of Bonao, in a fine valley of the same name, about twenty leagues from San Domingo, and ten from Fort Conception. Here they made their headquarters, at the house of Pedro Reguelme, one of the ringleaders.

Columbus immediately wrote to Miguel Ballester, the commander of Fort Conception, advising him to be on his guard. He empowered him to have an interview with Roldan, to offer him full pardon on condition of his immediate return to duty, and to invite him to repair to San Domingo to treat with the Admiral, under a solemn, and, if required, a written assurance of personal safety. At the same time he issued a proclamation, offering free passage to all who wished to return to Spain, in five vessels about to be put to sea, hoping by this means, to relieve the colony from all the idle and disaffected.

Ballester was an old and venerable man, grey-headed, and of a soldier-like demeanour; he was loyal, frank, and virtuous, of a serious disposition and great simplicity of heart. His appearance and character commanded the respect of the rebels; but they treated the proffered pardon with contempt, made many demands of an arrogant nature, and declared that in all further negotiations they would treat with no mediator but Carvajal, having had proofs of his fairness and impartiality in the course of their late communications with him at Xaragua.

This insolent reply was totally different from what the Admiral had been taught to expect. He now ordered the men of San Domingo to appear under arms, that he might ascertain the force with which he could take the field in case of necessity. A report was immediately circulated that they were to be led to Bonao, against the rebels; some of the inhabitants had relations, others friends, among the followers of Roldan; almost all were disaffected to the service; not above seventy men appeared under arms; one affected to be ill, another lame; there were not forty to be relied upon.

Columbus saw that a resort to arms would only serve to betray his own weakness and the power of the rebels. It was necessary to temporise, therefore, however humiliating such conduct might be deemed. His first care was to dispatch the five ships, which he had detained in port until he should receive the reply of Roldan. He was anxious that as many as possible of the discontented colonists should sail for Spain, before any commotion should take place. He wrote to the sovereigns an account of his late voyage, giving an enthusiastic description of the newly discovered continent, accompanied by a chart of the coast, and specimens of the pearls which he had procured from the natives.

He informed the sovereigns, also, of the rebellion of Roldan, and as the latter pretended it was only a quarrel between him and the Adelantado, he begged the matter might be investigated by their majesties, or by persons friendly to both parties. Among other judicious requests, he entreated that a man learned and experienced in the law might be sent out to officiate as judge over the island.

By this opportunity Roldan and his friends likewise sent letters to Spain, endeavouring to justify their rebellion, by charging Columbus and his brothers with oppression and injustice, and painting their whole conduct in the blackest colours. It would naturally be supposed that the representations of such men would have little weight in the balance against the tried merits and exalted services of Columbus; but they had numerous friends and relations in Spain to back them; Columbus was a foreigner, without influence in the court, and with active enemies near the sovereigns, ever ready to place his conduct in an unfavourable light.

The ships being dispatched, the Admiral resumed his negotiation with the rebels. As the burden of their complaint was the strict rule of his brother, who was accused of dealing out justice with a rigorous hand, he resolved to try the alternative of extreme lenity, and wrote a letter to Roldan, calling to mind past kindnesses, and entreating him, for the sake of his own reputation, which stood well with the sovereign, not to persist in his present insubordination. He again repeated his assurance that he and his companions might come to treat with him at San Domingo, under the faith of his word for the inviolability of their persons.

There was a difficulty as to who should be the bearer of this letter. The rebels had declared that they would receive no mediator but Alonzo Sanchez de Carvajal. Strong suspicions existed in the minds of many as to the integrity of that officer, from his transactions with the rebels at Xaragua, and his standing so high in their favour. Columbus, however, discarded all those suspicions, and confided implicitly in Carvajal, nor had he ever any cause to repent of his confidence.

A painful and humiliating negotiation was now carried on for several days, in the course of which Roldan had an interview with Columbus at San Domingo, and several letters passed between them. The rebels felt their power, and presumed, in consequence, to demand the most extravagant concessions. Miguel Ballester wrote at the same time to the Admiral, advising him to agree to whatever they might demand. He represented their forces as continually augmenting, and that the soldiers of his garrison were daily deserting to them, and gave it as his opinion that unless some compromise were speedily effected, and the rebels shipped off for Spain, not merely the authority, but even the person of the Admiral would be in danger; for though the hidalgoes and the immediate officers and servants about him would doubtless die in his service, yet he feared that the common people were but little to be depended upon.

Thus urged by veteran counsel, and compelled by circumstances, Columbus at length made an arrangement with the rebels, by which it was agreed that Roldan and his followers should embark for Spain, from the port of Xaragua, in two ships, which should be fitted out and victualled within fifty days. That they should each receive from the Admiral a certificate of good conduct, and an order for the amount of their pay up to the actual date.

It was a grievous circumstance to Columbus, that the vessels which should have borne his brother to explore the newly discovered continent had to be devoted to the transportation of this turbulent and worthless rabble; but he consoled himself with the idea that, the faction being once shipped off, the island would again be restored to tranquillity. The articles of arrangement being signed, Roldan and his followers departed for Xaragua, to await the arrival of the ships; and Columbus, putting his brother Don Diego in temporary command, set off with the Adelantado on a tour to visit the various fortresses, and restore order everywhere.

In the meanwhile, unavoidable delays took place in fitting out the ships, and they encountered violent storms in their voyage from San Domingo to Xaragua, so as to arrive there long after the stipulated time, and that in a damaged condition. The followers of Roldan seized upon this as a pretext to refuse to embark, affirming that the ships had been purposely delayed, and eventually sent in a state not seaworthy, and short of provisions. New negotiations were therefore set on foot and new terms demanded. It is probable that Roldan feared to return to Spain, and his followers were loth to give up their riotous and licentious life. In the midst of his perplexities Columbus received a letter from Spain, in reply to the earnest representations which he had made of the distracted state of the colony and of the outrages of these licentious men. It was written by his invidious enemy the Bishop Fonseca, superintendent of Indian affairs. It informed him that his representations of the alleged rebellion had been received, but that the matter must be suffered to remain in suspense, as the sovereigns would investigate and remedy it later.

This cold reply had the most disheartening effect upon Columbus, while it increased the insolence of the rebels, who saw that his complaints had little weight with the government. Full of zeal, however, for the prosecution of his discoveries, and of fidelity to the interests of the Crown, he resolved, at any sacrifice of pride or comfort, to put an end to the troubles of the island.

AUGUST

He departed, therefore, in the latter part of August, with two caravels, to the port of Azna, accompanied by several of the most important personages of the colony, to give Roldan a meeting. The latter, in this interview, conducted himself more like a conqueror exacting terms than a delinquent seeking pardon. Among other things, he demanded that such of his followers as chose to remain on the island should have lands assigned them, and that he should be reinstated in his office of Alcalde Mayor, or chief judge. Surrounded by doubt and danger, Columbus, a foreigner among a jealous people, an unpopular commander in a mutinous island, distrusted and slighted by the government he was seeking to serve, and creating suspicions by his very services, he knew not where to look for faithful advice, efficient aid, or candid judgment. He was alarmed, too, by symptoms of sedition among his own people, who talked of following the example of the rebels, and seizing upon the province of Higuey. Thus critically situated, he signed a humiliating capitulation with the rebels, trusting he should afterwards be able to convince the sovereigns it had been compulsory, and forced from him by the perils that threatened himself and the colony.

When Roldan resumed his office of Alcade Mayor, he displayed all the arrogance to be expected from one who had intruded himself into power by profligate means. Columbus had a difficult and painful task in bearing with the insolence of this man, and of the shameless rabble that returned, under his auspices, to San Domingo. In compliance with the terms of agreement he assigned them liberal portions of land and numerous Indian slaves, taken in the wars, and contrived to distribute them in various places, some in Bonao, others in different parts of the vega.

Having obtained such ample provisions for his followers, Roldan was not more modest in making demands for himself. Besides certain lands in the vicinity of Isabella which he claimed, as having belonged to him before his rebellion, he received a royal farm, called La Esperanza, in the Vega, and extensive tracts in Xaragua.

One of the first measures of Roldan as Alcalde Mayor was to appoint Pedro Reguelme, one of his most active confederates, alcalde of Bonao, an appointment which gave great displeasure to Columbus, being an assumption of power not vested in the office of Roldan. The Admiral received private information, also, that Reguelme, under pretext of erecting a farmhouse, was building a strong edifice on a hill, capable of being converted into a fortress; this, it was whispered, was done in concert with Roldan, by way of securing a stronghold in case of need. The Admiral immediately sent peremptory orders for Reguelme to desist from proceeding with the construction of the edifice.

Columbus had proposed to return to Spain, having experienced the inefficiency of letters in explaining the affairs of the island; but the feverish state of the colony obliged him to give up the intention. The two caravels were dispatched in October, taking such of the colonists

OCTOBER

as chose to return, and among them several of the partisans of Roldan, some of whom took Indian slaves with them, and others carried away the daughters of caciques, whom they had beguiled from their homes and families.

Columbus wrote by this opportunity to the sovereigns, giving it as his opinion that the agreement he had made with the rebels was by no means obligatory on the Crown, having been, in a manner, extorted by violence. He repeated his request that a learned man might be sent out as judge, and desired, moreover, that discreet persons might be appointed to form a council. Finding age and infirmity creeping upon him, he began to think of his son Diego as an active coadjutor, being destined to succeed to his offices. He was a page at court in Spain, but grown to man's estate, and capable of entering into the important concerns of life; he begged, therefore, that he might be sent out to assist him.

Some months later reports reached Columbus that four ships had anchored at the western part of the island, a little below Jacmel, apparently with the design of cutting dyewoods and carrying off the natives for slaves. They were commanded by Alonzo de Ojeda, hot-headed and bold-hearted cavalier. Knowing the daring and adventurous spirit of this man, the Admiral was disturbed at his visiting the island in this clandestine manner. To call him to account, however, required a man of spirit and address. No one seemed fitter for the purpose than Roldan. He was as daring as Ojeda, and of a more crafty character. An expedition of this kind would occupy the attention of himself and his partisans, and divert them from any schemes of mischief.

Roldan gladly undertook the enterprise. He had nothing further to gain by sedition, and was anxious to secure his ill-gotten possessions by public services, which should atone for past offences. Departing from San Domingo, with two caravels, he arrived on the 26th of September within two leagues of the harbour where the vessels of Ojeda were anchored. Here, landing with five-and-twenty resolute men, he intercepted Ojeda, who was on an

SEPTEMBER

excursion several leagues from his ships, and demanded his motives for landing on that remote and lonely part of the island, without first reporting his arrival to the Admiral. Ojeda replied that he had been on a voyage of discovery, and had put in there in distress, to repair his ships and obtain provisions. On further inquiry it appeared that Ojeda had happened to be in Spain at the time that the letters arrived from Columbus, giving an account of his discovery of the coast of Paria, accompanied by specimens of the pearls to be found there. Ojeda was a favourite with Bishop Fonseca, and obtained a sight of the letter and the charts and maps of the route of Columbus. He immediately conceived the idea of an expedition to those parts, in which he was encouraged by Fonseca, who furnished him with copies of the papers and charts, and granted him a letter of license, signed by himself, but not by the sovereigns.

Ojeda fitted out four ships at Seville, assisted by many eager and wealthy speculators; and in this squadron sailed Amerigo Vespucci, a Florentine merchant, well acquainted with geography and navigation, who eventually gave his name to the whole of the New World[1]. The expedition sailed in May, 1499. The adventurers arrived on the southern continent, and ranged along it, from two hundred leagues east of the Orinoco to the Gulf of Paria. Guided by the charts of Columbus, they passed through this gulf and through the *Boca del Drago*, kept along westward to Cape de la Vela, visiting the island of Margarita, and the adjacent continent, and discovering the gulf of Venezuela. They had subsequently touched at the Caribbean Islands, where they had fought with the fierce natives and made many captives, with the design of selling them in the slave markets of Seville. From thence they had sailed for Hispaniola to procure supplies, having performed the most extensive voyage hitherto made along the shores of the New World.

Ojeda assured Roldan that he intended, as soon as his ships were ready, to go to San Domingo and pay his homage to the Admiral. Trusting to this assurance, and satisfied with the information he had obtained, Roldan sailed for San Domingo

[1] From his christian name we derive the word AMERICA.

to make his report. Nothing, however, was farther from the intention of Ojeda than to keep his promise. As soon as his ships were ready for sea, he sailed round to the coast of Xaragua. Here he was well received by the Spaniards resident in that province, among whom were many of the late comrades of Roldan.

Knowing the rash and fearless character of Ojeda, and finding that there were jealousies between him and the Admiral, they made complaints of the injustice of the latter, whom they accused of withholding from them the arrears of their pay. Ojeda, who knew the tottering state of the Admiral's favour at court, and felt secure in the powerful protection of Fonseca, immediately proposed to put himself at their head, march at once to San Domingo, and oblige the Admiral to satisfy their just demands. The proposition was received with transport by some of the rebels; but others demurred, and a furious brawl ensued, in which several were killed and wounded on both sides; the party for the expedition to San Domingo remained triumphant.

Fortunately for the peace and safety of the Admiral, Roldan, who had received news of the movements of Ojeda, arrived in the neighbourhood at this critical juncture with a band of resolute followers, and was reinforced on the following day by his old confederate, Diego de Escobar with additional forces. Ojeda retired to his ships; a long course of manoeuvring took place between these well-matched adversaries, each striving to gain an advantage of the other. Ojeda at length was obliged to abandon the coast, and made sail for some other island to make up his cargo of Indian slaves.

The followers of Roldan took great merit to themselves for their unwonted loyalty in driving Ojeda from the island; and expected that their good conduct would be amply rewarded. Looking upon their leader as having everything in his gift, they requested him to share among them the fine province of Cahay, adjoining to Xaragua.

Roldan, who was now anxious to establish a character of adherence to the law, declined acceding to their wishes, until sanctioned by the Admiral; but, to soothe their impatence, he shared among them the lands which had been granted to him in Xaragua.

Columbus was at Fort Conception, with an inconsiderable force, when he heard of a plot to kill Roldan. This was planned by Hernando de Guevara, cousin to Adrian de Moxica, and a cavalier of noble family. Roldan, hearing of the plot of Guevara, banished him to the province of Cahay. The latter soon returned and meditated revenge. He was arrested and sent to the fortress of San Domingo. When de Moxica heard that his cousin had been arrested, he decided, not merely to rescue Guevara, but to kill Roldan and the Admiral.

Columbus saw that his safety depended upon prompt and vigorous measures. Taking with him ten trusty servants, all well armed, he came suddenly upon the conspirators in the night, seized Moxica and several of his principal confederates, and bore them off to Fort Conception. Resolving to set an example that should strike terror into the factions, he ordered that the instigator, Moxica, should be hanged on the top of the fortress. The latter entreated to be allowed a confessor. A priest was sent for. The miserable culprit, who had been so daring in rebellion, lost all courage at the near approach of death. He delayed and hesitated in his confession, as if hoping, by whiling away time, to give a chance for rescue. Instead of confessing his own sins he began to accuse others, until Columbus, losing all patience, in his mingled indignation and scorn, ordered the wretch to be flung from the battlements.

This sudden act of severity was promptly followed up. Pedro Reguelme was taken, with several of his confederates, in his ruffian-den at Bonao, and conveyed to the fortress of San Domingo. The conspirators fled for the most part to Xaragua, where they were pursued by the Adelantado, seconded by Roldan, and hunted out of all their old retreats. Thus in a little while the power of faction was completely subdued.

Columbus considered this happy event as brought about by the special intervention of Heaven, and gives in proof of it an instance of one of those visionary fancies by which he seems to have had at times when his mind was troubled by illness or anxiety. In the preceding winter, during the height of his cares and troubles, he had sunk into a state of despondency. In one of his gloomy moods he heard, he says, a voice which thus addressed him: "O man of little faith! fear nothing, be not cast down. I will provide for thee. I will take care of thee." On that very day, he adds, he received intelligence of the discovery of a number of gold mines.

The troubles and dangers which had surrounded him were breaking away, and order was coming out of confusion. He now looked forward to the prosecution of his grand enterprises, the exploring the coast of Paria, and the establishment of a pearl fishery in its waters. How illusive were his hopes! At this very moment those events were maturing that were to overwhelm him with distress, strip him of his honours, and render him comparatively a wreck for the remainder of his days!

CHAPTER XII

FRESH INTRIGUES IN THE SPANISH COURT AGAINST COLUMBUS—BOBADILLA IS APPOINTED TO EXAMINE HIS CONDUCT—THE ARRIVAL OF BOBADILLA AT SAN DOMINGO.

WHILE Columbus had been involved in a series of difficulties in the factious island of Hispaniola, his enemies had been successful in undermining his reputation in the court of Spain. Every vessel that returned from the New World came freighted with complaints, representing the character and conduct of Columbus and his brothers in the most odius point of view, insinuating that they were foreigners, who had nothing but their own interest and gratification in view. It was even alleged that Columbus intended to cast off all allegiance to Spain, and either to make himself sovereign of the countries he had discovered, or to yield them into the hands of some other power; a slander which, however extravagant, was calculated to startle the jealous mind of Ferdinand.

The Bishop Fonseca, and other enemies of Columbus who were about the court, having continual access to the sovereigns, were enabled to place everything urged against him in the strongest point of view, while they destroyed the force of his vindications. There was an incessant drain upon the mother country for the support of the colony. Was this compatible, they asked, with the extravagant pictures he had drawn of the wealth of the island and its golden mountains, in which he had pretended to find the Ophir of ancient days, the source of the riches of King Solomon? They inferred that he had either deceived the sovereigns by exaggerations or grossly wronged them by malpractices, or that he was totally incapable of the duties of government.

For the purpose of irritating the pride of the King, every man who returned from the colony was encouraged to put in claims for arrears of pay withheld by Columbus, or losses sustained in his service. A gang of the disorderly ruffians who had been shipped off, to free the island from their seditions, found their way to the court at Granada. They followed the King when he rode out, filling the air with complaints, and clamouring for their pay. About fifty of them assembled one day in the main court of the Alhambra, under the royal apartments, holding up bunches of grapes as the meagre diet to which they were reduced by their poverty, and by the cruel deceits of Columbus. Seeing the two sons of the Admiral pass by, who were pages to the Queen, they followed them with imprecations. "There go," cried they, "the whelps of him who discovered the land of vanity and delusion, the grave of Spanish hidalgoes!"

The incessant repetition of falsehood will gradually wear its way into the most candid mind. Isabella herself began to entertain doubts respecting the conduct of Columbus. If he and his brothers were upright, they might be injudicious; and mischief is often produced in government through error of judgment than iniquity of design. Isabella doubted, but the jealous Ferdinand felt convinced. He had never regarded Columbus with real cordiality, and since he had ascertained the importance of his discoveries, had regretted the extensive powers he had vested in his hands. He now resolved to send out some person to investigate the affairs of the colony, and, if necessary for its safety, to assume the command. This measure had actually been decided upon and the papers drawn out early in 1499; but, from various reasons, had been postponed. It is probable Isabella opposed so harsh a step against a man for whom she entertained an ardent gratitude and high admiration. The arrival of the ships with the late followers of Roldan brought matters to a crisis. The King listened entirely to the representations of the rebels, and a circumstance took place which, for a time, suspended the friendship of Isabella, the great safeguard of Columbus.

The followers of Roldan brought with them a number of slaves, some of which Columbus had been compelled to grant them by the articles of capitulation, others had been conveyed away quietly. The gifts and transfers of these unhappy beings were all represented as voluntary acts of Columbus. The sensibility of Isabella as a woman, and her dignity as a Queen, were instantly in arms. "What right," exclaimed she, indignantly, "has the Admiral to give away my vassals?" She immediately ordered all the Indians to be restored to their homes; and she commanded that those which had formerly been sent to Spain by the Admiral should be sought out and re-shipped to Hispaniola. Unfortunately for Columbus, at this very juncture, in one of his letters he advised the continuance of Indian slavery for some time longer, as a measure important to the welfare of the colony. This contributed to heighten the indignation of Isabella, and induced her no longer to oppose the sending out a commissioner to investigate his conduct, and, if necessary, to supersede him in command.

The person chosen for this most momentous office was Don Francisco de Bobadilla, an officer of the royal household. He is represented by some as a very honest and religious man; by others, and with apparent justice, as needy, passionate, and ambitious—three powerful objections to his acting as judge in a case where the utmost caution and candour were required, and where he was to derive wealth and power from the conviction of one of the parties.

AUGUST

Bobadilla arrived at San Domingo on the 23rd of August, 1500. Before entering the harbour he learnt, from a canoe which came off from the shore, that the Admiral and the Adelantado were absent in the interior of the island, and Don Diego in command. He was told of the recent insurrection of Moxica, and the punishments which had followed. Seven of the rebels had been hanged that week, and five more were in the fortress of San Domingo, condemned to suffer the same fate. Among these were Pedro Reguelme, the factious alcalde of Bonao, and Fernando de Guevara, a young cavalier. As the vessels entered the river, Bobadilla beheld on either bank a gibbet, with the body of a Spaniard hanging on it. He considered all these circumstances as conclusive proofs of the alleged cruelty of Columbus.

The report had already circulated in the city, that a commissioner had arrived to make inquisition into the late troubles. Many hastened on board the ship to pay early court to this public censor; and as those who sought to secure his favour were those who had most to fear from his scrutiny, it is evident that the nature of their communications was generally unfavourable to the Admiral. In fact, before Bobadilla landed, if not before he arrived, the culpability of the Admiral was decided in his mind. He acted accordingly. He made proclamation at the church door, in presence of Don Diego and the other persons in authority, of his letters patent, authorising him to investigate the rebellion and proceed against delinquents; and in virtue of these he demanded that Guevara, Reguelme, and the other prisoners should be delivered up to him.

Don Diego declared he could do nothing of the kind without the authority of the Admiral, and requested a copy of the letters patent, that he might send it to his brother. This Bobadilla refused, and added, that since the office he proclaimed appeared to have no weight, he would see what effect there was in the name of governor. On the following day, therefore, he had another royal patent read, investing him with the government of the islands, and of *Terra firma;* an authority which he was only to have assumed on absolute proof of the delinquency of Columbus. This letter being read, he again demanded the prisoners, and was again refused, Don Diego observing that they were held in obedience to the Admiral, to whom the sovereigns had granted letters of a higher nature.

Bobadilla now produced a mandate from the Crown, ordering Columbus and his brothers to deliver up all fortresses, ships, and other royal property; and another, ordering that the arrears of wages due to all persons in the royal service should be immediately paid, and the Admiral compelled to pay the arrears of those to whom he was individually accountable.

This last document was received with shouts by the multitude, to many of whom long arrears were due, in consequence of the poverty of the treasury. Flushed with his growing importance and popularity, Bobadilla again demanded the prisoners, and receiving the same reply, he proceeded to the fortress and made a formal demand of them of the alcayde Miguel Diaz. The latter refused to surrender them to any one but the Admiral. Upon this the whole spirit of Bobadilla was aroused. He assembled the sailors of the ships and the rabble of the place, marched them to the prison, broke open the door, which readily gave way, while some put up ladders to scale the walls. The alcayde, Miguel Diaz, and Don Diego de Alvarado appeared on the battlements with drawn swords, but offered no resistance. The fortress, having no garrison, was easily carried, and the prisoners were borne off in triumph, and given in custody to an alguazil.

Such was the entrance into office of Francisco de Bobadilla, and he continued his career in the same spirit, acting as if he had been sent out to degrade the Admiral, not to inquire into his conduct. He took up his residence in the house of Columbus, seized upon his arms, gold, plate, jewels, books, letters, and most secret manuscripts, giving no account of the property seized, paying out of it the wages of those to whom the Admiral was in arrears, and disposing of the rest as if already confiscated to the Crown. To increase his favour with the people, he proclaimed a general license for twenty years to seek for gold, exacting merely one-eleventh for government, instead of a third, as heretofore. At the same time he used the most unqualified language in speaking of Columbus, hinted that he was empowered to send him home in chains, and declared that neither he nor any of his lineage would ever again be permitted to govern the island.

CHAPTER XIII

COLUMBUS ARRESTED, PUT IN IRONS—AND SENT TO SPAIN.

WHEN Columbus received tidings at Fort Conception of the high-handed proceedings of Bobadilla, he considered them the unauthorised act of some rash adventurer; but the proclamation of his letters patent, which immediately took place throughout the island, soon convinced him he was acting under authority. He endeavoured then to persuade himself that Bobadilla was sent out to exercise the functions of chief judge, in compliance with the request contained in one of his own letters to the sovereigns, and that he was perhaps intrusted with provisional powers to inquire into the late troubles of the island. All beyond these powers he tried to believe were mere assumptions and exaggerations of authority, as in the case of Aguado. His consciousness of his own services and integrity, and his faith in the justice of the sovereigns forbade him to think otherwise. He proceeded to act on this idea; writing temperate and conciliatory letters to Bobadilla, cautioning him against his precipitate measures, while he endeavoured by counter proclamations to prevent the mischief he was producing.

Messengers soon arrived, however, who delivered to him a royal letter of credence, commanding him to give implicit faith and obedience to Bobadilla, and they gave him, at the same time, a summons from the latter to appear before him immediately at San Domingo. This laconic letter from the sovereigns struck at once at the root of his dignity and power; he made no longer any hesitation or demur, but departed alone and almost unattended to obey the peremptory summons of Bobadilla. The latter, in the meantime, had made a bustle of preparation and mustered the troops, affecting to believe a vulgar rumour that Columbus had called on the caciques of the vega to aid him in resisting the commands of the government. He moreover arrested Don Diego, threw him in irons, and confined him on board of a caravel, without assigning any cause for his imprisonment.

No sooner did he hear of the arrival of Columbus than he gave orders to put him also in irons, and to confine him in the fortress.

This outrage to a person of such dignified and venerable appearance, and such eminent merit, seemed for a time to shock even his enemies. When the irons were brought, every one present shrunk from the task of putting them on him, either out of a sentiment of compassion at so great a reverse of fortune, or out of habitual reverence for his person. To fill the measure of ingratitude meted out to him, it was one of his own servants that volunteered to rivet his fetters.

Columbus conducted himself with characteristic magnanimity under the injuries heaped upon him. He looked beyond this shallow agent, Bobadilla, and all his petty tyranny, to the sovereigns who had employed him. It was their injustice and ingratitude alone that could wound his spirit; and he felt assured that when the truth came to be known they would blush to find how greatly they had wronged him. With this proud assurance, he bore all present indignities in silence. He even wrote, at the demand of Bobadilla, a letter to the Adelantado, who was still in Xaragua, at the head of an armed force, exhorting him to submit quietly to the will of the sovereigns. Don Bartholomew immediately complied.

Relinquishing his command, he hastened peacefully to San Domingo, and, on arriving, experienced the same treatment with his brothers, being put in irons, and confined on board of a caravel. They were kept separate from each other, and no communication permitted between them. Bobadilla did not see them himself, nor did he allow others to visit them; and they were kept in total ignorance of the crimes with which they were charged, and the proceedings that were instituted against them.

The old scenes of the time of Aguado were now renewed with tenfold virulence. All the old charges were revived, and others added, still more extravagant in their nature. Columbus was accused of having prevented the conversion of the Indians, that they might be sold as slaves; with having secreted pearls collected on the coast of Paria, and kept the sovereigns in ignorance of the nature of his discoveries there, in order to exact new privileges from them. Even the late tumults were turned into matters of accusation, and the rebels admitted as evidence. The well-merited punishments inflicted upon certain of the ringleaders were cited as proofs of a cruel and revengeful disposition, and a secret hatred of Spaniards. Guevara, Reguelme, and their fellow-convicts were discharged almost without the form of a trial. Roldan, from the very first, had been treated with confidence by Bobadilla; all the others whose conduct had rendered them liable to justice received either a special acquittal or a general pardon.

Bobadilla had now collected testimony sufficient, as he thought, to insure the condemnation of the prisoners, and his own continuance in command. He determined, therefore to send home the Admiral and his brothers in chains, in the vessels which were ready for sea, with the inquest taken in their case, and private letters enforcing the charges made against them.

San Domingo now swarmed with men from the dungeon. Every base spirit which had been overawed by Columbus and his brothers, when in power, now hastened to revenge itself upon them when in chains. The most injurious slanders were loudly proclaimed in the streets, libels were posted up at the corners to taunt them with the exultings of the rabble.

The charge of conducting the prisoners to Spain was given to Alonzo de Villejo, an officer who was in the employ of Bishop Fonseca. He was instructed, on arriving at Cadiz, to deliver his prisoners into the hands of the Bishop, which circumstance has caused a belief that Fonseca was the secret instigator of all these violent proceedings. Villejo, however, was a man of honourable character and generous feelings, and showed himself superior to the low malignity of his patrons. When he arrived with a guard to conduct the Admiral from the prison to the ship, he found him in chains, in a state of deep despondency. So violently had he been treated, and so savage were the passions let loose against him, he had begun to fear he should be sacrificed without an opportunity of being heard, and that his name would go down to posterity sullied with imputed crimes.

When the officer entered with the guard, he thought it was to conduct him to the scaffold. "Villejo," said he, mournfully, "whither are you taking me?" "To the ship, your excellency, to embark," replied the other. "To embark!" repeated the Admiral, earnestly. "Villejo, do you speak the truth?" "By the life of your excellency," replied the honest officer, "it is true!" With these words the Admiral was comforted, and felt as one restored from death to life.

OCTOBER

The caravels set sail early in October, bearing off Columbus, shackled like the vilest of culprits, amidst the scoffs and shouts of a miscreant rabble, who took a brutal joy in heaping insults on his venerable head, and sent curses after him from the island he had so recently added to the civilised world. Fortunately the voyage was favourable and of moderate duration, and was rendered less irksome to Columbus by the conduct of those to whom he was given in custody. The worthy Villejo, as well as Andreas Martin, the master of the caravel, felt deeply grieved at his situation, and always treated him with profound respect and assiduous attention. They would have taken off his irons, but to this he would not consent. "No," said he, proudly, "their majesties commanded me by letter to submit to whatever Bobadilla should order in their name; by their authority he has put upon me these chains; I will wear them until they shall order them to be taken off, and I will afterwards preserve them as relics and memorials of the reward of my services."

"He did so," adds his son Fernando, in his history; "I saw them always hanging in his cabinet, and he requested that when he died they might be buried with him!"

CHAPTER XIV

HIS ARRIVAL AND MEETING WITH THE SOVEREIGNS—APPOINTMENT OF OVANDO TO REPLACE BOBADILLA.

THE arrival of Columbus at Cadiz, a prisoner, and in chains, produced almost as great a sensation as his triumphant return from his first voyage. A general burst of indignation arose in Cadiz, and in the powerful and opulent Seville, which was immediately echoed throughout all Spain. No one stopped to reason on the subject. It was sufficient to be told that Columbus was brought home in chains from the world he had discovered.

The tidings reached the court of Granada, and filled the halls of the Alhambra with murmurs of astonishment. On the arrival of the ships at Cadiz, Andreas Martin, the captain, had permitted Columbus to send off letters privately by express. The admiral, full of his wrongs, but ignorant how far they had been authorised by the sovereigns, forbore to write to them. He sent a long letter, however, to a lady of the court, high in favour with the Queen, and who had been nurse to Prince Juan. It contained an ample vindication of his conduct, couched in eloquent and dignified and touching language. When it was read to the noble-minded Isabella, and she found how grossly Columbus had been wronged and the royal authority abused, her heart was filled with mingled sympathy and indignation.

However Ferdinand might have secretly felt disposed against Columbus, the momentary tide of public sentiment was not to be resisted. He joined with his generous Queen in her reprobation of the treatment of the Admiral. Without waiting to receive any documents that might arrive from Bobadilla, they sent orders to Cadiz that the prisoners should be instantly set at liberty and treated with all distinction, and that two thousand ducats should be advanced to Columbus to defray the expenses of his journey to court. They wrote him a letter at the same time, expressing their grief at all that he had suffered, and inviting him to Granada.

The loyal heart of Columbus was cheered by this letter from his sovereigns. He appeared at court, not as a man ruined and disgraced, but richly dressed, and with an honourable retinue. He was received by their majesties with unqualified favour and distinction. When the Queen beheld this venerable man approach, and thought on all that he had suffered, she was moved to tears. Columbus had borne up firmly against the stern conflicts of the world; he had endured with lofty scorn the injuries and insults of ignoble men, but he possessed strong and quick sensibility. When he found himself thus kindly received, and beheld tears in the benign eyes of Isabella, his long-suppressed feelings burst forth; he threw himself upon his knees, and for some time could not utter a word.

Ferdinand and Isabella raised him from the ground, and endeavoured to encourage him by the most gracious expressions. As soon as he regained his self-possession he entered into an eloquent and high-minded vindication of his loyalty, and the zeal he had ever felt for the glory and advantage of the Spanish crown; if at any time he had erred, it had been, he said, through inexperience in the art of governing, and through the extraordinary difficulties by which he had been surrounded.

There was no need of vindication on his part. He stood in the presence of his sovereigns a deeply injured man, and it remained for them to vindicate themselves to the world from the charge of ingratitude towards their most deserving subject. They expressed their indignation at the proceedings of Bobadilla, which they disavowed, as contrary to his instructions; they promised that he should be immediately dismissed from his command, and Columbus reinstated in all his privileges and dignities, and indemnified for the losses he had sustained.

He expected, of course, to be immediately sent back in triumph to San Domingo, as Viceroy and Admiral of the

Indies; but in this he was doomed to experience a disappointment, which threw a gloom over the remainder of his days. The fact was that Ferdinand, however he may have disapproved of the violence of Bobadilla, was secretly well pleased with its effects. It had produced a temporary exclusion of Columbus from his high offices, and the politic monarch determined, in his heart, that he should never be restored to them. He had long repented having vested such great powers and prerogatives in any subject, particularly in a foreigner; but at the time of granting them he had no idea of the extent of the countries over which they would be exercised. Recent discoveries, made by various individuals, showed them to be almost boundless.

Vicente Yañez Pinzon, of the brave and intelligent family of navigators that had sailed with Columbus in his first voyage, had lately crossed the line, and explored the shores of the southern continent as far as Cape St. Augustine. Diego Lepe, another bold navigator of Palos, had doubled that Cape, and beheld the continent stretching away out of sight, to the southwest. The report of every discoverer put it beyond a doubt that these countries must be inexhaustible in wealth, as they appeared to be boundless in extent. Yet over all these Columbus was to be Viceroy, with a share in their productions and the profits of their trade that must yield him an incalculable revenue. The selfish monarch appeared almost to consider himself outwitted in the arrangement he had made; and every new discovery, instead of increasing his feeling of gratitude to Columbus, seemed only to make him repine at the growing magnitude of his reward.

Another grand consideration with the monarch was that Columbus was no longer indispensable to him. He had made his great discovery; he had struck out the route to the New World, and now any one could follow it. A number of able navigators had sprung up under his auspices, who were daily besieging the throne with offers to fit out expeditions at their own cost, and to yield a share of the profits to the Crown. Why should he, therefore, confer princely dignities and prerogatives for that which men were daily offering to perform gratuitously?

Such, from his after conduct, appears to have been the jealous and selfish policy which actuated Ferdinand in forbearing to reinstate Columbus in those dignities and privileges which had been solemnly granted to him by treaty. Plausible reasons, however, were given for delaying his reappointment. It was represented as advisable, therefore, to send some officer of talent and discretion to supersede Bobadilla, and to hold the government for two years, by which time all angry passions would be allayed and turbulent individuals removed. Columbus might then resume the command, with comfort to himself and advantage to the Crown. With this arrangement the Admiral was obliged to content himself.

The person chosen to supersede Bobadilla was Don Nicholas de Ovando. He is described as being of the middle size, with a fair complexion, a red beard, a modest look, yet a tone of authority; fluent in speech, courteous in manners, prudent, just, temperate, and of great humility. Such is the picture drawn of him by some of his contemporaries; yet he appears, from his actions, to have been plausible and subtle, as well as fluent and courteous; his humility concealed a great love of command; he was a merciless scourge to the Indians, and in his dealings with Columbus he was both ungenerous and unjust.

While the departure of Ovando was delayed by various circumstances, every arrival brought intelligence of the disastrous state of the island, under the administration of Bobadilla. The latter was not so much a bad, as an imprudent and a weak man. Imagining rigorous rule to be the rock on which his predecessor had split, he had at the very outset relaxed the reins of justice and morality, and, of course, had lost all command over the community.

Bobadilla sold the farms and estates of the Crown at low prices, and granted universal permission to work the mines, on paying only an eleventh of the produce to government. To prevent any diminution in the revenues it became necessary to increase the quantity of gold collected. His constant exhortation to the Spaniards was, to produce large quantities of gold.

"Make the most of your time," he would say, "there is no knowing how long it will last," alluding to the possibility of his being speedily recalled.

The colonists acted up to his advice, and so hard did they drive the poor natives that the eleventh yielded more revenue than had ever been produced by the third, under the government of Columbus.

The tidings of these abuses and of the wrongs of the natives grieved the spirit of Isabella, and induced her to urge the departure of Ovando. He was empowered to assume the command immediately on his arrival, and to send home Bobadilla by the return fleet. Hispaniola was to be the metropolis of the colonial government, which was to extend over the islands and *Terra Firma*. Ovando was to correct the late abuses, to revoke the improper licenses granted by Bobadilla, to lighten the burdens imposed upon the Indians, and to promote their religious instruction. He was, at the same time, to ascertain the injury sustained by Columbus in his late arrest and imprisonment, and the arrears of revenue that were due to him, that he might receive ample redress and compensation. The Admiral was to be allowed a resident agent in the island to attend to his affairs and guard his interests, to which office Columbus immediately appointed Alonzo Sanchez de Carvajal.

Among various decrees on this occasion we find the first trace of negro slavery in the New World. It was permitted to transport to the colony negro slaves born in Spain, the children and descendants of natives brought from Guinea, where the slave trade had for some time been carried on by the Spaniards and Portuguese. There are signal events in the course of history which sometimes bear the appearance of temporal judgments. It is a fact worthy of observation that Hispaniola, the place where this flagrant sin against nature and humanity was first introduced into the New World, had been the first to exhibit retribution.

FEBRUARY

The fleet appointed to convey Ovando to his government put to sea on the 13th of February, 1502. It was the largest armament that had yet sailed to the New World, consisting of thirty ships of various sizes, provided with all kinds of supplies for the colony. Twenty-five hundred souls embarked in this fleet. Ovando was allowed a brilliant retinue, a bodyguard of horsemen, and the use of silks, brocades, and precious stones, at that time forbidden by the laws of Spain.

FOURTH VOYAGE, 1502

CHAPTER XV

PREPARATIONS OF COLUMBUS FOR A FOURTH VOYAGE—TO SEA AGAIN—EXPOSED TO A VIOLENT TEMPEST AT SAN DOMINGO—HIS SEARCH FOR AN IMAGINARY STRAIT—DISCOVERY OF COSTA RICA AND PANAMA.

COLUMBUS remained in the city of Granada upwards of nine months, awaiting employment, and endeavouring to retrieve his affairs from the confusion into which they had been thrown.

Vasco da Gama had recently accomplished the long-attempted navigation to India by the Cape of Good Hope, and Pedro Alvarez Cabral, following in his track, had returned with his vessels laden with the precious merchandise of the East. The riches of Calicut were now the theme of every tongue. The discoveries of the savage regions of the New World had as yet brought but little revenue to Spain, but this route to the East Indies was pouring in immediate wealth on Portugal.

Columbus was roused to emulation, and trusted he could discover a route to those oriental regions more easy and direct than that of Vasco da Gama. According to his own observations, and the reports of other navigators, the coast of *Terra Firma* stretched far to the westward. The southern coast of Cuba, which he considered a part of the Asiatic continent, stretched onward towards the same point. The currents of the Caribbean Sea must pass between these lands. He was persuaded, therefore, that a strait must exist somewhere thereabout, opening into the Indian Sea. The situation in which he placed his conjectural strait was somewhere about what is at present called the Gulf of Darien. Could he but discover such a passage, and thus link the New World he had discovered with the opulent oriental countries of the old, he felt that he should make a magnificent close to his labours.

He unfolded his plan to the sovereigns, and, though it met with some narrow-minded opposition on the part of certain of the royal counsellors, it was promptly adopted, and he was empowered to fit out an armament to carry it into effect. He accordingly departed for Seville in April of 1502 to make the necessary preparations; but such were the delays caused by Fonseca and his agents, that it was not until the following month of May that he was able to put to sea.

Before sailing, he took measures to provide against any misfortune that might happen to himself in so distant and perilous an expedition. He caused copies to be made and authenticated of all the royal letters patent of his dignities and privileges; of his letter to the nurse of Prince Juan, containing a vindication of his conduct; and of two letters assigning to the bank of St. George, at Genoa, a tenth of his revenues to be employed in diminishing the duties on provisions in his native city. These two sets of documents he sent by different hands to his friend, Doctor Nicolo Odorigo, who had been Genoese ambassador to the court of Spain, requesting him to deposit them in some safe place at Genoa.

Age was rapidly making its advances upon Columbus when he undertook his fourth voyage of discovery. He was now about fifty-one years old. His constitution, originally vigourous in the extreme, had been impaired by hardships and exposures in every clime, and by the mental sufferings he had undergone. His intellectual powers alone retained their wonted energy, prompting him, at a period of life when most men seek rest, to sally forth with youthful ardour on the most toilsome and adventurous of enterprises. In this arduous voyage he was accompanied by his brother Don Bartholomew, who commanded one of the vessels.

MAY

Columbus sailed from Cadiz on the 9th of May, 1502. His squadron consisted of four caravels, the largest seventy tons, the smallest of fifty; the crews amounted in all to one hundred and fifty men. With this little armament and these slender barks he undertook the search after a strait, which, if found, must conduct him into the most remote seas, and lead to a complete circumnavigation of the globe. After touching at the Canaries, he had a prosperous voyage to the Caribbean Islands, arriving on the 15th of June at Mantinino, at present called Martinique. He had originally intended to steer to Jamaica, and from thence for the continent, in search of the supposed strait; but one of his vessels proving a slower ship, he bore away for Hispaniola to exchange it for one of the fleet which had recently taken out Ovando. This was contrary to his orders, which had expressly forbidden him to touch at Hispaniola until his return homewards, lest his presence should cause some agitation in the island; he trusted, however, the circumstances of the case would plead his excuse.

JUNE

Columbus arrived off the harbour of San Domingo at an unpropitious moment. The place was filled with the most virulent of his enemies, many of whom were in a high state of exasperation from recent proceedings which had taken place against them. The fleet which had brought out Ovando lay in the harbour, ready to put to sea; and was to take out Roldan, and many of his late adherents, some of whom were under arrest, and to be tried in Spain. Bobadilla was to embark in the principal ship, on board of which he had put an immense amount of gold, the revenue collected for the government during his administration, and which he confidently expected would atone for all his faults. Among the presents he intended for the sovereigns was one mass of virgin gold, which is famous in the old Spanish chronicles. It was said to weigh three thousand six hundred castillanos. Large quantities of gold had also been shipped in the fleet by the followers of Roldan, and other adventurers; the wealth gained by the sufferings of the unhappy natives.

It was on the 29th of June that Columbus arrived at the mouth of the river, and sent an officer on shore to explain to the Governor the purpose of his visit; he requested permission, moreover, to shelter his squadron in the river, as he apprehended an approaching storm. His request was refused by Ovando, who probably had orders from the sovereigns to that effect, and perhaps was further swayed by prudent considerations. Columbus then sent a second message, entreating that the sailing of the fleet might be delayed, as there were indubitable signs of an approaching tempest. This request was as fruitless as the preceding; the weather, to an inexperienced eye, was fair and tranquil, and the warning of the Admiral was treated with ridicule, as the prediction of a false prophet.

Columbus retired from the river, indignant at being denied relief and refused shelter in the very island which he had discovered. His crew murmured loudly at being excluded from a port of their own nation, where even strangers, under similar circumstances, would be admitted; and they repined at having embarked with a commander who was liable to such treatment. Columbus, feeling confident that a storm was at hand, kept his feeble squadron close to shore, and sought for shelter in some wild bay or river of the island.

In the meantime the fleet of Bobadilla set sail from San Domingo, and stood out confidently to sea. Within two days the predictions of Columbus were verified. One of those tremendous storms which sometimes sweep those latitudes had gradually gathered up and begun to blow. The little squadron of Columbus remained for a time tolerably well sheltered by the land, but the tempest increasing and the night coming on, with the unusual darkness, the ships lost sight of each other and were separated. The Admiral still kept close to the shore, and sustained no damage. The three other vessels ran out for sea-room, and for several days were driven about at the mercy of wind and wave, fearful each moment of shipwreck, and giving up each other as lost. The Adelantado, who commanded the worst vessel of the squadron, ran the most imminent hazard, and nothing but his brilliant seamanship enabled him to keep her afloat; he lost his longboat, and all the other vessels sustained more or less injury. At length, after various changes of fortune, they all arrived safely at Port Hermoso, to the west of San Domingo.

A different fate befell the other armament. The ship on board of which were Bobadilla, Roldan, and a number of the most inveterate enemies of Columbus, was swallowed up with all its crew, and with the celebrated mass of gold, and the principal part of the ill-gotten treasure gained by the miseries of the Indians. Many of the other ships were entirely lost, some returned to San Domingo in shattered condition, and only one was enabled to continue her voyage to Spain. That one, it is said, was the weakest of the fleet, and had on board of it four thousand pieces of gold, the property of the Admiral, remitted to Spain by his agent Carvajal. Both Fernando Columbus and the venerable historian Las Casas looked upon this event as one of those awful judgments which seem at times to deal forth temporal retribution. They notice the circumstance that, while the enemies of the Admiral were thus, as it were, before his eyes, swallowed up in the raging sea, the only ship enabled to pursue her voyage was the frail bark freighted with his property. Many of the superstitious seamen, who, from the sagacity displayed by Columbus in judging of the signs of the elements and his variety of scientific knowledge, looked upon him as endowed with supernatural powers, and fancied he had conjured up this storm by magic spells.

After repairing the damages sustained by his ships in the storm, Columbus steered for *Terra Firma;* but the weather falling perfectly calm, he was swept away to the northwest by the currents, until he arrived on the southern coast of Cuba.

JULY

The wind springing up fair, he resumed his course, and standing to the southwest, was enabled, on the 30th of July, to make the island of Guanaja, a few leagues distant from the coast of Honduras.

While the Adelantado was on shore at this island a canoe arrived, of an immense size, on board of which sat a cacique with his wives and children, under an awning of palm leaves. The canoe was paddled by twenty-five Indians, and freighted with various merchandise, the crude manufactures and natural productions of the adjacent countries. There were hatchets and other utensils of copper, with a kind of crucible for the melting of that metal. Various vessels neatly formed of clay, marble, and hard wood; mantles of cotton, worked and dyed with various colours, and many other articles which indicated a superior degree of art and civilisation than had hitherto been discovered in the New World.

The Indians, as far as they could be understood, informed the Admiral that they had come from a country rich, cultivated, and industrious, situated to the west, and urged him to steer in that direction. Well would it have been for Columbus had he followed their advice. Within a day or two he would have arrived at Yucatan; the discovery of Mexico and the other opulent countries of New Spain would have necessarily followed, the Southern Ocean would have been disclosed to him, and a succession of splendid discoveries would have shed fresh glory on his declining age, instead of its sinking amidst gloom, neglect, and disappointment.

The Admiral's whole mind, however, was at present intent upon discovering the supposed strait that was to lead him to the Indian Ocean. He sailed, therefore, southerly for some mountains which he described not many leagues distant, made Cape Honduras, and from thence proceeded easterly, sailing against contrary winds, and struggling with the currents which sweep that coast. There was an almost incessant tempest, with heavy rain and awful thunder and lightning. His vessels were strained so that their seams opened, the sails and rigging were torn, and the provisions damaged by the rain and the leakage. The sailors were exhausted with fatigue and harassed with terror. Several times they confessed their sins to each other, and prepared for death.

During a great part of this time Columbus suffered extremely from the gout, and his complaint was aggravated by watchfulness and anxiety. His illness did not prevent his attending to his duties; he had a small cabin or roundhouse constructed on the stern, from whence, even when confined to his bed, he could keep a lookout, and regulate the sailing of the ships.

Many times he was so ill that he thought his end approaching, and his anxious mind was distressed at the thoughts that his brother, Don Bartholomew was exposed to the same dangers and hardships. Often, too, his thoughts reverted to his son Diego, and the cares and misfortunes into which his death might plunge him. At length, after struggling for upwards of forty days to make a distance of about seventy leagues, he arrived, on the 14th of September, at a cape where the coast made a sudden bend, and turned directly south. Doubling this cape, he had immediately an easy wind, and swept off with flowing sail, in consequence of which he gave it the name of *Gracias a Dios*, or, Thanks to God.

SEPTEMBER

For three weeks he continued coasting what is at present called the Mosquito Bank, in the course of which a boat with its crew was swallowed up by the sudden swelling of a river. He had occasional interviews with the natives, but a mutual distrust prevailed between them and the Spaniards. The Indians were frightened at seeing a notary of the fleet take out pen, ink, and paper, and proceed to write down the information they were communicating; they supposed he was working some magic spell, and to counteract it they scattered a fragrant powder in the air, and burnt it, so that the smoke should be borne towards the Spaniards. The superstitious seamen looked upon these counter charms with equal distrust. They suspected the people of this coast to be great enchanters, and that all the delays and hardships they had experienced were in consequence of the ships being under some evil spell wrought by their magic arts. Even Columbus appears to have been tinctured with this superstition, which, indeed, is characteristic of the age. On the 5th of October Columbus arrived at what is at present called Costa Rica, or the Rich Coast, from the gold and silver mines found in after years among its mountains. Here he began to find ornaments of pure gold among the natives. These increased in quantity when he came to what has been called the coast of Veragua[1], where he

OCTOBER

[1] Today known as Panama.

was assured that the richest mines were to be found. In sailing along these coasts he received repeated accounts of a great kingdom in the west, called Ciguare, at the distance of several days' journey, where, as far as he could understand the imperfect explanations of his interpreters, the inhabitants wore crowns and bracelets and anklets of gold, and employed it in embroidering their garments and ornamenting and embossing their furniture. They were armed also, like the Spaniards, with swords, bucklers, and cuirasses, and were mounted on horses. The country was described also as being commercial, with seaports, in which ships arrived armed with cannon. Above all, Columbus understood that the sea continued round to this kingdom of Ciguare, and that ten days beyond it was the Ganges.

These were evidently rumours of the distant kingdom of Mexico, imperfectly interpreted to Columbus, and shaped and coloured by his imagination. He concluded that this country must be some province belonging to the Grand Khan, and must lie on the opposite side of a peninsula, and that he would soon arrive at a strait leading into the Indian Sea, which washed its shores. The supposed vicinity of the Ganges caused no surprise, as he had adopted the opinion of certain ancient philosophers who gave the world a smaller circumference than was generally imagined.

With these erroneous but ingenious ideas, Columbus continued to press forward in search of the imaginary strait, contending with adverse winds and currents, and meeting with great hostility from the natives; for the Indians of these coasts were fierce and warlike, and many of the tribes are supposed to have been of Carib origin. At sight of the ships the forests would resound with yells and war-whoops, with wooden drums, and on landing the shores would be lined with savage warriors, armed with clubs and lances, and swords of palm wood.

At length, having discovered and named Puerto Bello, and continued beyond Cape Nombre de Dios, Columbus arrived at a small and narrow harbour, to which he gave the name of *El Retrete*, or The Cabinet. Here he had reached the point to which Bastides, an enterprising voyager, coasting from the eastward, had recently explored. Whether Columbus knew or not of the voyage of this discoverer does not clearly appear, but here he was induced to give up all further attempt to find the strait. The seamen were disheartened by the constant opposition of the winds and currents, and by the condition of the ships, which were pierced in all parts by the teredo or worm so destructive in the tropical seas. They considered themselves still under an evil spell, worked by the Indian sorcerers, and the commanders remonstrated against forcing their way any farther in spite of the elements, with ships so crazed and leaky. Columbus yielded to their solicitations and determined to return to the coast of Veragua, and search for the mines which were said to abound there.

Here, then, ended the lofty anticipations which had elevated him above all mercenary views in his struggle along these perilous coasts, and had given a heroic character to the early part of his voyage. The subsequent discovery of the Pacific Ocean, bathing the opposite shores of that narrow isthmus, has proved that a great part of his theory was well founded.

THE LANDING OF COLUMBUS ON ESPANIOLA

(After one of the first contemporary pamphlets, printed at Basle, 1494.)

Claimed by many authorities to be drawn by Columbus on a letter sent to a friend in Spain—following his landing.

CHAPTER XVI

TROUBLES WITH THE NATIVES AT PANAMA—FINDS GOLD —VOYAGE TO JAMAICA—SHIPWRECKED—DIEGO MENDEZ LEAVES FOR HELP.

ON the 5th of December Columbus sailed from El Retrete, to return westward in search of the gold mines of Veragua. He had not proceeded far, however, when the wind suddenly veered to the west, the point from whence, for three months, he had been wishing it to blow, but from whence it now came only to contradict him. In a little while it became so variable and furious as to baffle all seamanship. For nine days the vessels were tossed about at the mercy of a raging tempest, in an unknown sea, and often exposed to the awful perils of the shore. The sea, according to the description of Columbus, boiled at times like a cauldron; at other times it ran in mountain waves, covered with foam. At night, the raging billows sparkled with luminous particles which made them resemble great surges of flame. For a day and a night the heavens glowed like a furnace, with incessant flashes of lightning; while the loud claps of thunder were often mistaken by the mariners for signal guns of distress from their foundering companions. During the whole time there was such a deluge of rain that the seamen were almost drowned in their open vessels.

DECEMBER

In the midst of this wild tumult of the elements they beheld a new object of alarm. The ocean in one place became strangely agitated. The water was whirled up into a kind of pyramid or cone, while a livid cloud, tapering to a point, bent down to meet it. Joining together, they formed a column, which rapidly approached the ships, spinning along the surface of the deep, and drawing up the waters with a rushing sound. The frightened mariners, when they beheld this waterspout advancing towards them, despaired of averting it by human means, and began to repeat certain passages from St. John the Evangelist. The waterspout passed close by their ships without injuring them, and they attributed their escape to the miraculous efficacy of their quotations from the Scriptures.

An interval of calm succeeded, but even this afforded but little consolation to the tempest-tossed mariners; they looked upon it as deceitful, and beheld with alarm great numbers of sharks, so abundant and ravenous in those latitudes, roaming about the ships. Among the superstitions of the seas is the belief that these voracious fish have not only the faculty of smelling dead bodies at a distance, but have a presentiment of their prey, and keep about vessels which have sick persons on board, or which are in danger of being wrecked.

For three weeks longer they continued to be driven to and fro by changeable and tempestuous winds, endeavouring to make a distance of merely thirty leagues, insomuch that Columbus gave this line of seaboard the name of *La Costa de los Contrastes*, or the Coast of Contradictions. At length, to his great joy, he arrived on the day of Epiphany (the 6th of January) on the coast of Veragua, and anchored in a river, to which, in honour of the day, he gave the name of *Belen* or Bethlehem.

JANUARY

The natives of the neighbourhood manifested the same fierce and warlike character that generally prevailed along this coast. They were soon conciliated, however, and brought many ornaments of fine gold to traffic; but assured the Admiral that the mines lay near the river Veragua, which was about two leagues distant. The Adelantado had an interview with Quibian, the cacique of Veragua, who afterwards visited the ships. He was a stern warrior, of tall and powerful frame, and taciturn and cautious character. A few days afterwards the Adelantado, attended by sixty-eight men well armed, proceeded to explore the Veragua, and seek its reputed mines. They ascended the river about a league and a half, to the village of Quibian, which was situated on a hill. The cacique descended with a numerous train of his subjects, unarmed, and took his seat on a great stone, which one of his attendants drew out of the river. He received his guests with courtesy, for the lofty, vigorous, and iron form of the Adelantado, and his resolute demeanour, were calculated to inspire awe and respect in an Indian warrior. Though his jealousy was evidently awakened by the intrusion of the Spaniards into his territories, yet he readily furnished Don Bartholomew with guides to conduct him to the mines.

These guides led the Adelantado and his men six leagues into the interior, among thick forests of lofty and magnificent trees, where they told them the mines were situated. In fact, the whole soil appeared to be impregnated with gold, and the Spaniards collected a considerable quantity from the surface of the earth, and from among the roots of the trees. From hence the Adelantado was conducted to the summit of a high hill, which overlooked an immense extent of country, with various villages, and the guides assured him that the whole land, to the distance of twenty days' journey westward, abounded in gold.

Another expedition of Don Bartholomew along the coast, westward, was equally satisfactory; and the reports which he brought of golden tracts of country, together with the rumours of a rich and civilised kingdom in the interior, and the erroneous idea with respect to the vicinity of the Ganges, all concurred to produce a new illusion in the ardent mind of Columbus. He fancied that he had actually arrived at the *Aurea Chersonesus*, from whence, according to Josephus, the gold had been procured for the building of the temple of Jerusalem.

APRIL

Towards the end of April Columbus set sail from the coast of Veragua, and was determined to make his way to Hispaniola; but it was necessary, before sailing across for that island, to gain a considerable distance to the east, to avoid being swept away far below their destined port by the currents. The pilots and mariners, who had not studied the navigation of these seas with an equally experienced and observant eye, fancied, when Columbus sailed along the coast to the east, that he intended to proceed immediately to Spain, and murmured loudly at the madness of attempting so long a voyage, with ships now destitute of stores and consumed by the worms. The Admiral did not impart his reasons, for he was disposed to make a mystery of his routes, seeing the number of private adventurers daily crowding into his track.

Continuing along the coast eastward, he was obliged to abandon one of the caravels in the harbour of Puerto Bello, being so pierced by the teredo that it was impossible to keep her afloat. He then proceeded about ten leagues beyond Point Blas, near to what is at present called the Gulf of Darien, and which he supposed to be the province of Mangi, in the territories of the Grand Khan. Here he bade farewell to the mainland, and stood northward on the 1st of May, in quest of Hispaniola. Notwithstanding all his precautions, however, he was carried so far west by the currents as to arrive, on the 30th of May, among the cluster of islands called the Queen's Gardens, on the south side of Cuba. During this time his crews had suffered excessively from hunger and fatigue. They were crowded into two caravels, little better than mere wrecks, and which were scarcely kept afloat by incessant labour at the pump. They were enfeebled by scanty diet, and dejected by a variety of hardships. A violent storm on the coast of Cuba drove the vessels upon each other, and shattered them to such a degree that the Admiral, after struggling as far as Cape Cruz, gave up all further attempt to navigate them to Hispaniola, and stood over in search of a secure port on the island of Jamaica. Here, on the 24th of June, they anchored in a harbour, to which the Admiral gave the name of *Port San Gloria*.

MAY

JUNE

Seeing that his ships were no longer capable of standing the sea, and were in danger of foundering even in port, Columbus ran them aground, within bowshot of the shore, where they were fastened together side by side. They soon filled with water. Thatched cabins were then erected at the prow and stern to shelter the crews, and the wreck was placed in the best possible state of defence; thus castled in the sea, Columbus trusted to be able to repel any sudden attack of the natives, and at the same time to keep his men under proper restraint.

No one was permitted to go ashore without special license, and the utmost precaution was taken to prevent any offence being given to the Indians, who soon swarmed to the harbour with provisions, as any exasperation of them might be fatal to the Spaniards in their present forlorn situation. Two persons were appointed to superintend all bargains, and the provisions thus obtained were divided every evening among the people. As the immediate neighbourhood, however, might soon be exhausted, the zealous and intrepid Diego Mendez made a tour in the interior, accompanied by three men, and made arrangements for the caciques at a distance to furnish daily supplies at the harbour, in exchange for European trinkets. He returned in triumph, in a canoe which he had purchased from the Indians, and which he had freighted with provisions, and through his able arrangement the Spaniards were regularly supplied.

The immediate wants of his people being thus provided for Columbus revolved, in his anxious mind, the means of getting from this island. His ships were beyond the possibility of repair; there was no hope of a chance ship arriving to his relief, on the shores of a savage island, in an unfrequented sea. At length a mode of relief occurred to him, through the means of this same Diego Mendez, whose courage and loyalty he had so often proved. He took him aside to sound him on the subject, and Mendez himself has written an account of this interesting conversation, which is full of character.

> "Diego Mendez, my son," said the venerable Admiral, "of all those who are here, you and I alone know the great peril in which we are placed. We are few in number, and these savage Indians are many, and of fickle and irritable natures. On the least provocation they may throw firebrands from the shore and consume us in our straw-thatched cabins. The arrangement which you have made for provisions, and

which at present they fulfil so cheerfully, they may capriciously break tomorrow, and may refuse to bring us anything; nor have we the means of compelling them. I have thought of a remedy, if it meets your views. In this canoe which you have purchased, some one may pass over to Hispaniola, and procure a ship, by which we shall all be delivered from this great peril. Tell me your opinion on the matter."

"Señor," replied Diego Mendez, "I well know our danger to be far greater than is easily conceived; but as to passing to Hispaniola in so small a vessel as a canoe, I hold it not merely difficult, but impossible, since it is necessary to traverse a gulf of forty leagues, and between islands where the sea is impetuous and seldom in repose. I know not who there is would venture upon so extreme a peril."

Columbus made no reply; but from his looks, and the nature of his silence, Mendez plainly perceived himself to be the person whom the Admiral had in view. Resuming, therefore, the conversation: "Señor," said he, "I have many times put my life in peril to save you and my comrades, and God has hitherto preserved me in a miraculous manner. There are, nevertheless, murmurers who say that your excellency intrusts to me every affair wherein honour is to be gained, while there are others in company who would execute them as well as I. I beg, therefore, that you would assemble the people, and propose this enterprise, to see if any one will undertake it, which I doubt. If all decline, I will then come forward and risk my life in your service, as I have many times done already."

The Admiral willingly agreed to the wishes of the worthy Mendez; for never was simple vanity accompanied by more generous and devoted zeal.

On the following morning the crew was accordingly assembled, and the proposition made. Every one drew back, pronouncing it the height of rashness. Upon this, Diego Mendez stepped forward.

> "Señor," said he, "I have but one life to lose, yet I am willing to venture it for your service, and for the good of all here present; and I trust in the protection of God, which I have experienced on so many other occasions."

Columbus embraced this zealous follower, who immediately set about preparing for the expedition. Drawing his canoe on shore, he put on a false keel, and nailed weatherboards along the bow and stern, to prevent the sea from breaking over it. He then painted it with a coat of tar, furnished it with a mast and sail, and put in provisions for himself, a Spanish comrade, and six Indians.

In the meanwhile, Columbus wrote a letter to Ovando, Governor of Hispaniola, begging that a ship might immediately be sent to bring him and his men to that island, and he wrote another to the sovereigns, entreating for a ship to convey them from Hispaniola to Spain. In this letter he gave a comprehensive account of his voyage, and expressed his opinion that Veragua was the *Aurea Chersonesus* of the ancients. He supposed himself to have reached the confines of the dominions of the Grand Khan, and offered, if he lived to return to Spain, to conduct a mission thither to instruct that potentate in the Christian faith. What an instance of soaring enthusiasm and irrepressible enterprise is exhibited here! At the time he was indulging these visions, and proposing new and romantic enterprises, he was broken down by age and infirmities, racked by pain, confined to his bed, and shut up in a wreck on the coast of a remote and savage island.

The dispatches being ready, Diego Mendez embarked with his Spanish comrade and his six Indians, and coasted the island eastward. Their voyage was toilsome and perilous. When arrived at the end of the island, they were suddenly surrounded and taken prisoners by the Indians, who carried them three leagues into the interior, where they determined to kill them. A dispute arising about the division of the spoils, they agreed to settle it after the Indian fashion, by a game of ball. While thus engaged, Diego Mendez escaped, regained his canoe, and made his way back to the harbour in it alone, after fifteen days' absence. Nothing daunted by the perils and hardships he had undergone, he offered to depart immediately, on a second attempt, provided he could be escorted to the end of the island by an armed force.

His offer was accepted and Bartholomew Fiesco, a Genoese, was associated with Mendez. Each was to have a canoe, with six Spaniards and ten Indians under his command. On reaching Hispaniola, Fiesco was to return immediately to Columbus bringing him the news that his messenger had arrived safely. Diego Mendez, however, was to proceed to San Domingo, and, after purchasing and dispatching a ship, was to depart for Spain with the letter to the sovereigns.

All arrangements being made, the Indians placed in the canoes a supply of cassava bread, and each his calabash of water. The Spaniards, besides their provisions, had each his sword and target. The Adelantado, with an armed band, kept pace with them along the coast until they reached the end of the island, where, waiting for three days until the weather was perfectly serene, they launched forth on the broad bosom of the sea. The Adelantado remained watching them until they became mere specks on the ocean, and the evening hid them from his view, and then returned to the harbour.

CHAPTER XVII

MUTINY OF PORRAS—THREAT OF FAMINE—ECLIPSE OF THE MOON

MONTHS elapsed, and nothing was heard of Mendez. The Spaniards, enfeebled by past sufferings, crowded in close quarters, in a moist and sultry climate, and reduced to a vegetable diet, to which they were unaccustomed, became extremely sickly, and their maladies were heightened by anxiety and suspense. Day after day and week after week they kept a wistful lookout upon the sea for the expected return of Fiesco, flattering themselves that every Indian canoe, gliding at a distance, might be the harbinger of deliverance. It was all in vain; and at length they began to fear that their messengers had perished. Some gradually sank into despondency; others became peevish and impatient, and, in their unreasonable heat, railed at their venerable and infirm commander as the cause of all their misfortunes.

Among the officers of Columbus were two brothers, Francisco and Diego Porras, relations of the royal treasurer Morales. To gratify the latter, the Admiral had appointed one of them captain of a caravel, and the other notary and accountant-general of the expedition. They were vain and insolent men, and, like many others whom Columbus had benefited, requited his kindness with the blackest ingratitude. Mingling with the people, they assured them that Columbus had no intention of returning to Spain, having in reality been banished thence by the sovereigns. Hispaniola, they said, was equally closed against him, and it was his design to remain in Jamaica until his friends could make interest at court to procure his recall. As to Mendez and Fiesco, they had been sent to Spain by Columbus on his own private concerns; if this were not the case, why did not the promised ship arrive? Why did not Fiesco return? Or, if the canoes had really been sent for succour, the long time that had elapsed without tidings gave reason to believe that they had perished by the way. In such case their only alternative would be to take Indian canoes, and endeavour to reach Hispaniola; but there was no hope of persuading the Admiral to do this; he was too old and too infirm to undertake such a voyage.

By these insidious suggestions they gradually prepared the people for revolt, assuring them of the protection of their own relatives in Spain, and of the countenance of Ovando and Fonseca, if not of the favour of the sovereigns themselves, who had shown their ill-will towards Columbus by stripping him of part of his dignities and privileges.

JANUARY

On the 2nd of January, 1504, the mutiny broke out. Francisco Porras suddenly entered the cabin, where Columbus was confined to his bed by the gout, reproached him vehemently with keeping them in that desolate place to perish, and accused him of having no intention to return to Spain. The Admiral raised himself in bed, and, maintaining his calmness, endeavoured to reason with the traitor; but Porras was deaf to all argument. "Embark immediately, or remain, in God's name!" he cried, with a voice that resounded all over the wreck. "For my part, I am for Castile! those who choose may follow me!"

This was the signal. "For Castile! for Castile!" was heard on every side. The mutineers sprang upon the most conspicuous parts of the vessel, brandishing their weapons, and, amidst the uproar, the voices of some desperadoes were heard menacing the life of the Admiral.

Columbus, ill and infirm as he was, leaped out of bed, and tottered forth to pacify the mutineers, but was forced back into his cabin by some of his faithful adherents. The Adelantado sallied forth, lance in hand, and planted himself in a situation to take the whole brunt of the assault. It was with the greatest difficulty that several of the loyal part of the crew could restrain his fury, and prevail upon him to relinquish his weapon, and retire to the cabin of his brother.

The mutineers, being entirely unopposed, took ten canoes, which the Admiral had purchased from the Indians; others, who had not been concerned in the mutiny, joined them, through fear of remaining behind, when so reduced in number; in this way, forty-eight abandoned the Admiral. Many of the sick crawled forth from their cabins, and beheld their departure with tears and lamentations, and would gladly have accompanied them had their strength permitted.

Porras coasted with his squadron of canoes to the eastward, landing occasionally and robbing the natives, pretending to act under the authority of Columbus, that he might draw on him their hostility. Arrived at the east end of the island, he procured several Indians to manage the canoes, and then set out on his voyage across the gulf. The Spaniards had scarcely proceeded four leagues when the wind came ahead, with a swell of the sea that threatened to overwhelm the deeply laden canoes. They immediately turned for land, and, in their alarm, threw overboard the greater part of their effects. The danger still continuing, they drew their swords, and compelled most of the Indians to leap into the sea. The latter were skilful swimmers, but the distance to land was too great for their strength; if, however, they at any time took hold of the canoes to rest themselves and recover breath, the Spaniards, fearful of their overturning the slight barks, would stab them, or cut off their hands. Some were thus slain by the sword; others sunk exhausted beneath the waves; eighteen perished miserably; and none survived but a few who had been retained to manage the canoes.

Having reached the shore in safety, Porras and his men waited until the weather became favourable, and then made another effort to cross to Hispaniola, but with no better success. They then abandoned the attempt in despair, and returned westward, towards the harbour, roving from village to village, living upon the provisions of the Indians, which they took by force, if not readily given, and conducting themselves in the most licentious manner. If the natives remonstrated they told them to seek redress at the hands of the Admiral, whom, at the same time, they represented as the implacable foe of the Indian race, and bent upon gaining a tyrannical sway over their island.

In the meantime Columbus, when abandoned by the mutineers, and left in the wreck with a mere handful of sick and desponding men, exerted himself to the utmost to restore this remnant to an efficient state of health and spirits. He ordered that the small stock of biscuit which remained, and the most nourishing articles of the provisions furnished by the Indians, should be appropriated to the invalids; he visited them, individually, cheered them with hopes of speedy deliverance, and promised that on his return to Spain he would intercede with the sovereigns, that their loyalty might be munificently rewarded. In this way, by kind and careful treatment and encouraging words, he succeeded in restoring them from a state of sickness and despondency, and rendering them once more fit for service.

Scarcely, however, had the little garrison of the wreck recovered from the shock of the mutiny, when it was menaced by a new and appalling evil. The scanty number of the Spaniards prevented them from foraging abroad for provisions, and rendered them dependent on the voluntary supplies of the natives. The latter began to grow negligent. The European trinkets, once so inestimable in their eyes, by becoming common, had sunk in value, and were almost treated with indifference. The arrangements made by Diego Mendez were irregularly attended to, and at length entirely disregarded. Many of the caciques had been incensed by the conduct of Porras and his followers, which they supposed justified by the Admiral; others had been secretly instigated by the rebels to withhold provisions, in hopes of starving Columbus and his people, or of driving them from the island.

The horrors of famine began to threaten the terrified crew, when a fortunate idea presented itself to Columbus. From his knowledge of astronomy, he ascertained that within three days there would be a total eclipse of the moon, in the early part of the night. He summoned, therefore, the principal caciques to a grand conference, appointing for it the day of the eclipse. When all were assembled, he told them, by his interpreter, that he and his followers were worshippers of a Deity, who lived in the skies, and held them under his protection. That this great Deity was incensed against the Indians, who had refused or neglected to furnish his faithful worshippers with provisions, and intended to chastise them with famine and pestilence. Lest they should disbelieve this warning, a signal would be given that very night in the heavens. They would behold the moon change its colour, and gradually lose its light; a token of the fearful punishment which awaited them.

Many of the Indians were alarmed at the solemnity of this prediction, others treated it with derision; all, however, awaited with solicitude the coming of the night. When they beheld a black shadow stealing over the moon, and a mysterious gloom gradually covering the whole face of nature, they were seized with the utmost consternation. Hurrying with provisions to the ships, and throwing themselves at the feet of Columbus, they implored him to intercede with his God to withhold the threatened calamities, assuring him that thenceforth they would bring him whatever he required. Columbus retired to his cabin, under pretence of communing with the Deity, the forests and shores all the while resounding with the howling of the savages. He returned shortly, and informed the natives that the Deity had deigned to pardon them, on condition of their fulfilling their promises; in sign of which he would withdraw the darkness from the moon.

When the Indians saw that planet restored presently to its brightness, and rolling in all its beauty through the firmament, they overwhelmed the Admiral with thanks for his intercession. They now regarded him with awe and reverence, as one in peculiar favour and confidence of the Deity, since he knew upon earth what was passing in the heavens. They hastened to propitiate him with gifts; supplies again arrived daily at the harbour, and from that time forward there was no want of provisions.

CHAPTER XVIII

DESERTED BY OVANDO—PORRAS IS TAKEN PRISONER—VOYAGE OF DIEGO MENDEZ TO HISPANIOLA—DELIVERANCE OF COLUMBUS FROM JAMAICA.

EIGHT months had now elapsed since the departure of Mendez and Fiesco, yet no tidings had been received of their fate. The hopes of the most sanguine were nearly extinct, and many, considering themselves abandoned and forgotten by the world, grew wild and desperate in their plans. Another conspiracy, similar to that of the brothers Porras, was on the point of breaking out, when one evening, towards dusk, a sail was seen standing towards the harbour. It was a small caravel, which kept out at sea, and sent its boat on shore. In this came Diego de Escobar, one of the late confederates of Roldan, who had been condemned to death under the administration of Columbus, and pardoned by his successor, Bobadilla. There was bad omen in such a messenger.

Escobar was the bearer of a mere letter of compliment and condolence from Ovando, accompanied by a barrel of wine and a side of bacon. The Governor expressed great concern at his misfortunes, and regret at not having in port a vessel of sufficient size to bring off himself and people, but promised to send one as soon as possible. Escobar drew off with the boat and kept at a distance from the wreck, awaiting any letters the Admiral might have to send in reply, and holding no conversation with any of the Spaniards. Columbus hastened to write to Ovando, depicting the horrors of his situation, and urging the promised relief. As soon as Escobar received this letter he returned on board of his caravel, which made all sail, and disappeared in the gathering gloom of the night.

The mysterious conduct of Escobar caused great wonder

and consternation among the people. Columbus sought to dispel their uneasiness, assuring them that vessels would soon arrive to take them away. In confidence of this, he said, he had declined to depart with Escobar, because his vessel was too small to take the whole, and had dispatched him in such haste that no time might be lost in sending the requisite ships. These assurances, and the certainty that their situation was known in San Domingo, cheered the hearts of the people, and put an end to the conspiracy.

Columbus, however, was secretly indignant at the conduct of Ovando, believing that he had purposely delayed sending relief, in the hopes that he would perish on the island, being apprehensive that, should he return in safety, he would be reinstated in the government of Hispaniola. He considered Escobar merely as a spy, sent by the Governor to ascertain whether he and his crew were yet in existence. Still, he endeavoured to turn the event to some advantage with the rebels. He sent two of his people to inform them of the promise of Ovando to send ships for his relief, and he offered them a free pardon and a passage to Hispaniola, on condition of their immediate return to obedience.

On the approach of the ambassadors, Porras came forth to meet them accompanied solely by a few of the ringleaders of his party, and prevented their holding any communication with the mass of his people. In reply to the generous offer of the Admiral, they refused to return to the wreck, but agreed to conduct themselves peaceably and amicably, on receiving a solemn promise that, should two vessels arrive, they should have one to depart in; should but one arrive, the half of it should be granted to them; and that, in the meantime, the Admiral should share with them the sea stores and articles of Indian traffic which remained in his possession. When it was observed that these demands were extravagant and inadmissible, they replied, that if they were not peaceably conceded they would take them by force; and with this menace they dismissed the ambassadors.

The conference was not conducted so privately but that

the rest of the rebels learnt the whole purport of the mission. Porras, seeing them moved by the offer of pardon and deliverance, resorted to the most desperate falsehoods to delude them. He told them that these offers of the Admiral were all deceitful; and that he only sought to get them into his power, that he might wreak on them his vengeance. As to the pretended caravel which had visited the harbour, he assured them that it was a mere phantasy, conjured up by the Admiral, who was deeply versed in magic. In proof of this he adverted to its arriving in the dusk of the evening; its holding communication with no one but the Admiral, and its sudden disappearance in the night. Had it been a real caravel, the crew would have sought to converse with their countrymen; the Admiral, his son, and brother would have eagerly embarked on board; at any rate, it would have remained a little while in port, and not have vanished so suddenly and mysteriously.

By these and similar delusions, Porras succeeded in working upon the feelings of his followers, and persuaded them that, if they persisted in their rebellion, they would ultimately triumph, and perhaps send home the Admiral in irons, as had once before been done from Hispaniola. To involve them beyond hope of pardon he marched them one day towards the harbour, with an intention of seizing upon the stores remaining in the wreck, and getting the Admiral in his power.

Columbus heard of their approach, but, being confined by his infirmities, sent Don Bartholomew to reason with them and endeavour to win them to obedience. The Adelantado, who was generally a man rather of deeds than words, took with him fifty men, well armed. Arriving near the rebels, he sent messengers to treat with them, but Porras forbade them to approach. The latter cheered his followers by pointing with derision to the pale countenances of their opponents, who were emaciated by recent sickness and long confinement in the wreck, whereas his men, for the most part, were hardy sailors, rendered robust by living in the open air. He assured them the followers of the Adelantado were mere household men, fair-weather troops, who could never stand before them.

Deluded by his words into a transient glow of courage, the rebels did not wait to be attacked, but rushed with shouts upon the enemy. Six of them had made a league to assault the Adelantado, but were so well received that he laid several of them dead at his feet. In the midst of the affray the Adelantado was assailed by Francisco Porras, who, with a blow of his sword, cleft his buckler and wounded the hand which grasped it. The sword remained wedged in the shield; and before it could be withdrawn the Adelantado closed upon Porras, grappled him, and being assisted by others, succeeded in taking him prisoner.

The rebels, seeing their leader a captive, fled in confusion, but were not pursued, through fear of an attack from the Indians, who had remained drawn up in battle array, gazing with astonishment at this fight between white men, but without offering to aid either party. The Adelantado returned in triumph to the wreck, with Porras and several other prisoners. Only two of his own men had been wounded, one of whom died. On the following day the rebels sent in a letter to the Admiral, confessing all their misdeeds, imploring pardon, and making a solemn oath of obedience, and imprecating the most awful curses on their heads should they break it. The Admiral saw, by the abject nature of the letter, how completely the spirit of these misguided men was broken; with his wonted magnanimity he pardoned their offences, merely retaining their ringleader, Francisco Porras, a prisoner, to be tried in Spain for his misdeeds.

It is proper here to give some account of the mission of Diego Mendez and Bartholomew Fiesco. When they had taken leave of the Adelantado, at the east end of the island of Jamaica, they continued all day in a direct course; there was no wind, the sky was without a cloud, and the sea, like a mirror, reflected the burning rays of the sun. The Indians who paddled the canoes would often leap into the water, to cool their glowing bodies and refresh themselves from their toil. At the going down of the sun they lost sight of land. During the night the Indians took turns, one half to row while the others slept. The Spaniards, in like manner, divided their forces; while some took repose, the others sat with their weapons in their hands, ready to defend themselves in case of any perfidy on the part of their savage companions.

Watching and toiling through the night, Diego Mendez was excessively fatigued on the following day; and, to add to his distress, he began to experience the torments of thirst; and the Indians, also parched with heat, had drained the contents of their calabashes. In proportion as the sun rose their misery increased, and was irritated by the prospect around them—nothing but water, while they were perishing with thirst. About mid-day, when their strength was failing them, the commander produced two small kegs of water, which he had probably reserved in secret for such an extremity. Administering a cooling mouthful occasionally, he enabled the Indians to resume their toils. They held out the hopes of soon arriving at a small island, called Navasa, which lay directly in their way, about eight leagues distant from Hispaniola. Here they would find water to assuage their thirst, and would be able to take repose.

The night closed upon them without any sight of the island; they feared that they had deviated from their course; if so, they should miss the island entirely, and perish with thirst before they could reach Hispaniola. One of the Indians died of the accumulated sufferings of labour, heat, and raging thirst; others lay panting and gasping at the bottom of the canoes. Their companions were scarcely able to continue their toils. Sometimes they endeavoured to cool their parched palates by taking sea water in their mouths; but its briny bitterness only increased their thirst. One after another gave up, and it seemed impossible that they should live to reach Hispaniola.

The commander, by admirable management, had hitherto kept up this weary struggle with suffering and despair; but he, too, began to despond. Diego Mendez sat watching the horizon, which was gradually lighting up with those faint rays which precede the rising of the moon. As that planet arose, he perceived it to emerge from behind a dark mass elevated above the level of the ocean. It proved to be the island of Navasa, but so low and small and distant that, had it not been thus revealed by the rising moon, he would never have discovered it. He immediately gave the cry of "Land!" His almost expiring companions were roused to new life, and exerted themselves with feverish impatience. By the dawn of day they sprang on shore, and returned thanks to God for their deliverance. The island was a mere barren mass of rocks, but they found abundance of rain-water in hollow places. The Spaniards exercised some degree of caution in their drinking, but the poor Indians, whose toils had increased the fever of their thirst, gave way to a kind of frantic indulgence, of which several died upon the spot, and others fell dangerously ill.

After reposing all day on the island, where they made a grateful meal from shellfish gathered along the shore, they set off in the evening for Hispaniola, the mountains of which were distinctly visible, and arrived at Cape Tiburon on the following day.

Diego Mendez took six Indians of the island, and set off for San Domingo. After proceeding for eighty leagues against the currents, he was informed that the Governor had departed for Xaragua, fifty leagues distant. Still undaunted by fatigues and difficulties, he abandoned the canoe, and proceeded alone, on foot, through forests and over mountains, until he arrived at Xaragua, achieving one of the most perilous expeditions ever undertaken by a devoted follower for the safety of his commander.[1]

[1] Some brief notice of the further fortunes of Diego Mendez may be interesting to the reader.

When King Ferdinand heard of his faithful services, he bestowed rewards upon him, and permitted him to bear a canoe in his coat of arms, as a memento of his hardy enterprise. He continued devotedly attached to the Admiral, serving him zealously after his return to Spain, and during his last illness. Columbus retained a grateful and affectionate sense of his fidelity. On his death-bed he promised Mendez that he should be appointed principal Alguazil of the island of Hispaniola. The promise, however, was not performed by the heirs of Columbus. Mendez was afterwards engaged in various voyages of discovery, met with many vicissitudes, and died poor. In his last will he requested that his armorial bearing of an Indian canoe should

He found Ovando completely engrossed by wars with the natives. The Governor expressed great concern at the unfortunate situation of Columbus, and promised to send him immediate relief; but Mendez remained for seven months at Xaragua, vainly urging for that relief, or for permission to go to San Domingo in quest of it. The constant excuse of Ovando was that there were not ships of sufficient size on the island to bring off Columbus and his men. At length, by daily importunity, Mendez obtained permission to go to San Domingo, and await the arrival of certain ships which were expected. He immediately set out on foot; the distance was seventy leagues, and part of his toilsome journey lay through forests and mountains, infested by hostile and exasperated Indians. Immediately after his departure, Ovando dispatched from Xaragua the pardoned rebel, Escobar, on that reconnoitring visit which caused so much wonder and suspicion among the companions of Columbus.

If the Governor had really entertained hopes that, during the delay of relief, Columbus might perish in the island, the report brought back by Escobar must have completely disappointed him. No time was now to be lost, if he wished to claim any merit in his deliverance, or to avoid the disgrace of having totally neglected him. His long delay had already roused the public indignation, insomuch that suggestions had been made upon his conduct, even in the pulpits. Diego Mendez, also, had hired and victualled a vessel at the expense of Columbus, and was on the point of dispatching it. The Governor, therefore, exerted himself, at the eleventh hour, and fitted out a caravel, which he put under the command of Diego de Salcedo, the agent employed by Columbus to collect his rents in San Domingo. It was these two vessels which arrived at Jamaica shortly after the battle with Porras, and brought relief

---

be engraved on his tombstone, and under it the following words: "Here lies the honorable Cavalier, Diego Mendez; who served greatly the royal crown of Spain, in the conquest of the Indies, with Admiral Christopher Columbus, of glorious memory, who made the discovery; and afterwards by himself, in ships at his own cost."—W.I.

to the Admiral and his faithful adherents, after a long year of dismal confinement to the wreck.

On the 28th of June all the Spaniards embarked, friend and foe, on board of the vessels, and made sail joyfully for San Domingo; but, from adverse winds and currents, they did not arrive there until the 13th of August. Whatever lurking enmity there might be to Columbus in the place, it was overpowered by popular sympathy for his late disasters. Whatever had been denied to his merits was granted to his misfortunes; and even the envious, appeased by his present reverses, seemed to forgive him for having once been so triumphant.

JUNE

AUGUST

The Governor and the principal inhabitants came forth to meet him, and received him with signal distinction. He was lodged in the house of Ovando, who treated him with the utmost courtesy and attention; but there were too deep causes of jealousy and distrust between them for their intercourse to be cordial. Their powers, too, were so defined in their several patents as to clash with each other, and to cause questions of jurisdiction. Ovando assumed a right to take cognizance of all transactions at Jamaica, as happening within the limits of his government. He set at liberty the traitor Porras, and talked of punishing the followers of Columbus for the deaths of the mutineers whom they had slain in battle. Columbus, on the other hand, asserted the absolute jurisdiction given him by the sovereigns in his letter of instructions, over all persons who had sailed in his expedition, from the time of their departure from Spain until their return. The Governor heard him with great courtesy and a smiling countenance, but observed, that the letter gave him no authority within the bounds of his government. He relinquished the idea, however, of trying the faithful adherents of Columbus, and sent Porras to Spain, to be examined by the board which had charge of the affairs of the Indies.

CHAPTER XIX

AFFAIRS AT HISPANIOLA DURING THE ADMINISTRATION OF OVANDO—RETURN OF COLUMBUS TO SPAIN.

THE sojourn of Columbus at San Domingo was but little calculated to yield him satisfaction. He was grieved at the desolation of the island, through the oppressive treatment of the natives, and the horrible massacres which had taken place under the administration of Ovando. And here let us turn for a moment from pursuing the story of the Admiral, to notice some of the principal occurrences which had taken place in Hispaniola during his absence.

A great crowd of adventurers, of various ranks, had thronged the fleet of Ovando, all confidently expecting to make sudden fortunes. They had scarcely landed when they all hurried off to the mines, which were about eight leagues distant. The road swarmed like an anthill. Every one had his knapsack of biscuit and flour, and his mining implements on his shoulder. Those hidalgoes, or gentlemen, who had no servants to carry their burdens, were fain to bear them on their own backs, and lucky was he who had a horse for the expedition, for he would be able to bring back the greater load of treasure. They all set off in high spirits, eager who should first reach the golden land; thinking they had but to arrive at the mines, and gather gold as easily and readily as fruit from the trees. When they arrived, however, they found, to their dismay, that it required experience to discover the veins of ore; that the whole process of mining was exceedingly slow and toilsome, and its results precarious.

"Their labour," says Las Casas[1] "gave them a keen appetite

[1] An Italian writer who published an abridgement of the *Journal* of Columbus during 1747. No trace of the original *Journal* exists.

and quick digestion, but no gold." They soon exhausted their provisions and their patience, and returned murmuring along the road they had lately trod so exultingly. They arrived at San Domingo half famished, downcast, and despairing. Such is too often the case of those who ignorantly engage in mining; which, of all objects of speculation, is the most brilliant, promising, and fallacious. Poverty soon fell upon these misguided men. Some wasted away, and died broken-hearted; others were hurried off by raging fevers; so that there soon perished upwards of a thousand men.

Ovando was reputed a man of great prudence and sagacity, and he certainly took several judicious measures for the regulation of the island and the relief of the colonists; but his policy was fatal to the natives. When he had been sent out to supersede Bobadilla, the Queen, shocked at the cruel bondage which had been inflicted on the Indians, had pronounced them all free. The consequence was, they immediately refused to labour in the mines.

Ovando, in 1503, represented that this entire liberty granted to the natives was not merely ruinous to the colony but detrimental to themselves, as it produced habits of idleness, profligacy, and neglect of all religion. The sovereigns permitted, therefore, that they should be obliged to labour moderately, if essential to their well-being, but that they should be paid regularly and fairly, and instructed in religion on certain days, and that all compulsory measures should be tempered with persuasion and kindness. Under cover of this hired labour, thus intended for the health of soul and body, more intolerable toil was exacted from them and more horrible cruelties inflicted than in the worst days of Bobadilla.

Many perished from hunger, or sank under the lash; many killed themselves in despair. Even those who survived the exacted terms of labour and were permitted to return to their homes, which were often sixty and eighty leagues distant, were dismissed so worn down by toil and hardship, and so scantily furnished with provisions, that they perished by the way. Some sank down and died by the side of a brook, others under the shade of a tree, where they had crawled for shelter from the sun. "I found many dead on the road," wrote Las Casas; "others gasping under the trees, and others in the pangs of death, faintly crying, 'Hunger! hunger!'"

The wars of Ovando were equally desolating. To punish a slight insurrection in the province of Higuey, at the eastern end of the island, he sent his troops, who ravaged the country with fire and sword, showed no mercy to age or sex, put many to death with the most wanton, ingenious, and horrible tortures, and brought off the brave Cotabanama, one of the five sovereign caciques of the island, in chains to San Domingo, where he was ignominiously hanged by Ovando for the crime of defending his territory and his native soil against usurping strangers.

But the most atrocious act of Ovando, and one that must heap odium on his name wherever the woes of the gentle natives of Haiti create an interest, was the punishment he inflicted on the province of Xaragua for a pretended conspiracy. The exactions of tribute, in this once happy and hospitable province, had caused occasional quarrels between the inferior caciques and the Spaniards; these were magnified by alarmists, and Ovando was persuaded that there was a deep-laid plot among the natives to rise upon their oppressors. He immediately set out for Xaragua, at the head of nearly four hundred well-armed soldiers, seventy of whom were steel-clad horsemen. He gave out that he was going on a visit of friendship, to make arrangements about the payment of tribute.

Behechio, the ancient cacique of the province, was dead, and his sister, Anacaona, had succeeded to the government. She came forth to meet Ovando, according to the custom of her nation, attended by her most distinguished subjects, and her train of damsels, waving palm branches, and dancing to the cadence of their popular areytos. All her principal caciques had been assembled to do honour to her guests, who for several days were entertained with banquets and national games and dances. In return for these exhibitions, Ovando invited Anacaona, with her beautiful daughter Higuenamota, and her principal subjects, to witness an exhibition by the cavalry in the public square. When all were assembled, the square crowded with unarmed Indians, Ovando gave a signal, and instantly the horsemen rushed into the midst of the naked and defenceless throng, trampling them under foot, cutting them down with their swords, transfixing them with their lances, and sparing neither age nor sex. Above eighty caciques had been assembled in one of the principal houses. It was surrounded by troops, the caciques were bound to the posts which supported the roof, and put to cruel tortures, until, in the extremity of anguish, they were made to admit the truth of the plot with which their Queen and themselves had been charged. When self-accusation had thus been tortured from them, a horrible punishment was immediately inflicted; fire was set to the house, and they all perished miserably in the flames.

As to Anacaona, she was carried to San Domingo, where the mockery of a trial was given her, in which she was found guilty, on the confessions wrung by torture from her subjects, and she was barbarously hanged, by the people whom she had so long and so signally befriended.

After the massacre at Xaragua the destruction of its inhabitants still went on; they were hunted for six months amidst the mountains, and their country ravaged by horse and foot, until, all being reduced to deplorable misery and abject submission, Ovando pronounced the province restored to order, and, in commemoration of his triumph, founded a town near the lake, which he called *Santa Maria de la Verdadera Paz*, St. Mary of the True Peace.

Such was the tragical fate of the beautiful Anacaona, once extolled as the Golden Flower of Haiti; and such the story of the delightful region of Xaragua, a place which the Europeans, by their own account, found a perfect paradise, but which, by their vile passions, they filled with horror and desolation.

* * *

Columbus found his own immediate concerns in great confusion. His rents and arrears were either uncollected, or he could not obtain a clear account and a full liquidation of them; and he complained that Ovando had impeded his agents in their management of his concerns. The continual misunderstandings which took place between him and the Governor, though always qualified on the part of the latter with courtly complaisance, induced Columbus to hasten his departure. He caused the ship in which he had returned from Jamaica to be repaired and fitted out, and another hired, in which he offered a passage to such of his late crew as chose to return. The greater part preferred to remain in San Domingo; as they were in great poverty, he relieved their necessities from his own purse, and advanced money to those who accompanied him, for the expenses of their voyage. All the funds he could collect were exhausted in these disbursements, and many of the men, thus relieved by his generosity, had been among the most violent of the rebels.

SEPTEMBER

On the 12th of September he set sail; but had scarcely left the harbour when the mast of his ship was carried away in a sudden squall. He embarked, therefore, with his family in the other vessel, commanded by the Adelantado, and sent back the damaged ship to port. Fortune continued to persecute him to the end of this, his last and most disastrous expedition. Throughout the voyage he experienced tempestuous weather, suffering, at the same time, the excruciating torments of the gout, until, on the 7th of November, his crazy and shattered bark anchored in the harbour of San Lucar[1]. From thence he proceeded to Seville, to enjoy a little tranquillity of mind and body, and to recruit his health after his long series of fatigues, anxieties, and hardships.

NOVEMBER

[1] In Spain.

CHAPTER XX

ILLNESS OF COLUMBUS AT SEVILLE—APPLICATION TO THE CROWN FOR RESTITUTION OF ALL HONOURS—DEATH OF ISABELLA—THE LAST ILLNESS AND DEATH OF CHRISTOPHER COLUMBUS.

THE residence of Columbus, during the winter, at Seville, has generally been represented as an interval of repose: never was honourable repose more merited, more desired, and less enjoyed. Care and sorrow were destined to follow him, by sea and land; and in varying the scene he but varied the nature of his afflictions. Since his memorable arrest by Bobadilla his affairs had remained in confusion, and his rents and dues had been but partially and irregularly collected, and were detained in intermediate hands. The last voyage had exhausted his finances and involved him in embarrassments. All that he had been able to collect of the money due to him in Hispaniola had been expended in bringing home many of his late crew, and, for the greater part, thc crown remained his debtor. The world thought him possessed of countless wealth, while in fact he was suffering a degree of penury.

In letters written at this time to his son Diego, he repeatedly urges to him the necessity of practising extreme economy until the arrears due to him should be paid. "I receive nothing of the revenue due to me," says he on another ocscaion, "but live by borrowing. Little have I profited by twenty years of toils and perils, since at present I do not own a roof in Spain. I have no resort but an inn; and, for the most times, have not wherewithal to pay my bill."

Being unable, from his infirmities, to go to court, he had to communicate with the sovereigns by letter, or through the intervention of friends, and exerted himself strenuously, but ineffectually, to draw their attention to the disastrous state of Hispaniola under the administration of Ovando, to obtain the restitution of his honours and the payment of his arrears, and, what seemed to lay equally near his heart, to obtain relief for his unfortunate seamen.

His letters were unregarded, or at least unanswered; his claims remained unsatisfied; and a cold indifference and neglect appeared to prevail towards him. All the tidings from the court filled him with uneasiness. Porras, the ringleader of the late faction, had been sent home by Ovando to appear before the council of the Indies, but the official documents in his cause had not arrived. He went at large, and being related to Morales, the royal treasurer, had access to people in place, and an opportunity of enlisting their opinions and prejudices on his side. Columbus began to fear that the violent scenes in Jamaica might, by the perversity of his enemies and the effrontery of the delinquents, be wrested into matters of accusation against him, as had been the case with the rebellion of Roldan.

The faithful and indefatigable Diego Mendez was at this time at court, and he trusted to his honest representations to counteract the falsehoods of Porras. Nothing can surpass the affecting earnestness and simplicity with which, in one of his letters, he declares his loyalty. "I have served their majesties," says he, "with as much zeal and diligence as if it had been to gain Paradise, and if I have failed in anything, it has been because my knowledge and powers went no further." Whilst reading this touching appeal we can scarcely realise the fact that it should be written by Columbus, the same extraordinary man who, but a few years before, had been idolised at this court as a benefactor, and received with almost royal honours.

His anxiety to have a personal interview with the sovereigns became every day more intense; he felt the inefficacy of letter writing; and, indeed, even that resource began to fail him, for the severity of his malady for a great part of the time deprived him of the use of his hands. He made repeated attempts to set off for the court; a litter was once actually at the door to convey him thither, but his increasing infirmities and the inclemency of the season obliged him to abandon the journey. In the meantime, the intrigues of his enemies appeared to be prevailing; the cold-hearted Ferdinand treated all his applications with indifference; on the justice and magnanimity of Isabella, alone, he relied for the re-dress of his grievances; but she lay dangerously ill. "May it please the Holy Trinity," says he, "to restore our sovereign Queen to health; for by her will everything be adjusted which is now in confusion." Alas! while writing that letter, his noble benefactress died.

The health of Isabella had long been undermined by repeated shocks of domestic calamities. The death of her only son, the Prince Juan; of her beloved daughter, the Princess Isabella; and of her grandson and prospective heir, the Prince Miguel, had been three cruel wounds. The desolation which walks through palaces does not admit the familiar sympathies and sweet consolations which alleviate the sorrows of common life. Isabella pined in state, amidst the obsequious homage of a court, surrounded by the trophies of a glorious and successful reign, and placed at the summit of earthly grandeur. A deep and incurable melancholy settled upon her, which undermined her constitution, and gave a fatal acuteness to her bodily maladies. After four months of illness, she died, on the 26th of November, 1504, at Medina del Campo, in the fifty-fourth year of her age; but long before her eyes closed upon the world, her heart had closed upon all its pomps and vanities. "Let my body," said she, in her will, "be interred in the monastery of San Francisco, in the Alhambra of the city of Granada, in a low sepulchre, with no other monument than a plain stone, and an inscription. But I desire and command, that if the King, my lord, should choose a sepulchre in any church or monastery in any other part or place of these my kingdoms, that my body be transported thither, and buried beside the body of his highness; so that the union we have enjoyed while living, and which, through the mercy of God, we hope our souls will experience in heaven, may be represented by our bodies in

NOVEMBER

the earth[1]."

The news of the death of Isabella reached Columbus while he was writing a letter to his son. He notices it in a postscript or memorandum, written in the haste and brevity of the moment, but in beautifully touching and mournful terms. "A memorial," he writes, "for thee, my dear son Diego, of what is at present to be done. The principal thing is to commend affectionately, and with great devotion, the soul of the Queen, our sovereign, to God. Her life was always catholic and pious, and prompt to all things in his holy service; for this reason we may rest assured that she is received into his glory, and beyond the cares of this rough and weary world. The next thing is, to watch and labour in all matters for the service of our sovereign, the King, and to endeavour to alleviate his grief. His majesty is the head of Christendom. Remember the proverb which says, when the head suffers, all the members suffer. Therefore all good Christians should pray for his health and long life; and we, who are in his employ, ought more than others to do this with all study and diligence."

It is impossible to read this letter without being moved by the simply eloquent yet artless language in which Columbus expresses his tenderness for the memory of his benefactress, his weariness under the gathering cares and ills of life, and his persevering and enduring loyalty towards the sovereign who was so ungratefully neglecting him.

The death of Isabella was a fatal blow to his fortunes. While she lived, he had everything to anticipate from her high sense of justice, her regard for her royal word, her gratitude for his services, and her admiration of his character. With her illness, however, his interests had languished; and when she died, he was left to the justice and generosity of Ferdinand!

[1] The dying command of Isabella has been obeyed. Washington Irving wrote in the first edition that he had seen her tomb in the royal chapel of the cathedral of Granada, in which her remains are interred with those of Ferdinand. "Their effigies, sculptured in white marble," he wrote, "lie side by side, on a magnificent sepulchre. The altar of the chapel is adorned with bas-reliefs representing the conquest and surrender of Granada".

During the remainder of the winter and a great part of the spring he remained at Seville, detained by painful illness. His brother, the Adelantado, who supported him with his accustomed fondness and devotion through all his trials, proceeded to court to attend to his concerns, taking with him the Admiral's younger son, Fernando, then aged about seventeen.

Among the persons whom Columbus employed at this time in his missions to the court was Amerigo Vespucci. He describes him as a worthy but unfortunate man, who had not profited as much as he deserved by his undertakings, and who had always been disposed to render him service.

MAY

It was not until the month of May that Columbus was able to accomplish his journey to court, which was at that time at Segovia. He, who but a few years before had entered the city of Barcelona in triumph, attended by the chivalry of Spain, and hailed with rapture by the multitude, now arrived at the gates of Segovia, a way-worn, melancholy, and neglected man; oppressed even more by sorrows than by his years and infirmities. When he presented himself at court he was made lamentably sensible of the loss of his protectress, the benignant Isabella. He met with none of that distinguished attention, that cordial kindness, that cherishing sympathy, which his unparalleled services and his recent sufferings had merited. Ferdinand, it is true, received him with many professions of kindness; but with those cold, ineffectual smiles which pass like wintry sunshine over the countenance, and convey no warmth to the heart.

Many months were passed by Columbus in painful and humiliating solicitation. His main object was to obtain the restitution of his high offices as Viceroy and Governor of the Indies: as to the mere claims for revenues and arrears, he considered them of minor importance, and nobly offered to leave them to the disposition of the King. His official dignities belonged to his reputation; they had been granted, also, by solemn treaty, and were not to be made a matter of arbitrament. As the latter, however, were precisely the claims which the jealous monarch was the least disposed to grant, they stood continually in the way of all arrangement. The whole matter was at one time referred to a tribunal called the *Junta de Descargos*, which had charge of the settlement of the affairs of the late Queen, but nothing resulted from their deliberations; the wishes of the King were too well known to be thwarted.

Columbus endeavoured to bear these delays with patience; but he had no longer the physical strength and the glorious anticipations which had once sustained him through his long application at this court. He was again confined to his bed by a return of the gout, aggravated by the irritations of his spirit. From this couch of anguish he addressed one more appeal to the justice of the King. He no longer petitioned for himself, but for his son Diego. He entreated that he might be appointed in his place to the government of which he had been so wrongfully deprived. "This," said he, "is a matter which concerns my honour; as to all the rest, do as your majesty thinks proper; give or withhold, as may be most for your interest, and I shall be content. I believe it is the anxiety caused by the delay of this affair which is the principal cause of my ill-health."

This petition was treated by Ferdinand with his usual evasions; he endeavoured to prevail upon Columbus and his son to waive their claims to paramount dignities in the New World, and accept, in place thereof, titles and estates in Spain. Columbus rejected all proposals of the kind with indignation, as calculated to compromise those titles which were the trophies of his achievements. He saw, however, that all further hope of redress from Ferdinand was vain. From the bed to which he was confined he addressed a letter to his constant friend, Diego de Deza, then Archbishop of Seville, expressive of his despair. "It appears," said he, "that his majesty does not think fit to fulfil that which he, with the Queen who is now in glory, promised me by word and seal. For me to contend to the contrary would be to contend with the wind. I have done all that I could do. I leave the rest to God, whom I have ever found propitious to me in my necessities."

In the midst of illness and despondency, when both life and hope were expiring in the bosom of Columbus, a new gleam was awakened, and blazed up for the moment with characteristic fervour. He heard with joy of the arrival from Flanders of King Philip and Queen Juana, to take possession of their throne of Castile. In the daughter of Isabella he trusted to find a patroness and a friend. King Ferdinand and all the court repaired to Loredo, to receive the youthful sovereigns. Columbus sent his brother, the Adelantado, to represent him, and wrote a letter to the King and Queen, lamenting his being prevented by illness from coming in person to manifest his devotion. He expressed a hope that he should receive at their hands a restitution of his honours and estates; and assured them that, though cruelly tortured at present by disease, he would yet be able to render them services, the like of which had never been witnessed.

Such was the last sally of his sanguine and unconquerable spirit; which, disregarding age and infirmities, and all past sorrows and disappointments, spoke from his dying bed with all the confidence of youthful hope, and talked of still greater enterprises, as if he had a long and vigourous life before him. The Adelantado took an affectionate leave of his brother, whom he was never to see again, and set out on his mission to the new sovereigns. He experienced the most gracious reception, and flattering hopes were given him that the claims of the Admiral would speedily be satisfied.

In the meantime, the cares and troubles of Columbus were drawing to a close. Immediately after the departure of the Adelantado his illness increased in violence. Finding that his end was approaching, he arranged all his earthly affairs, for the benefit of his successors. In a codicil made on the eve of his decease he enforced his original testament, constituting his son Diego his universal heir, entailing his honours and estates on the male line of his family, and providing for his brothers, Don Bartholomew and Don Diego. Other provisions were made for the foundation of churches, the relief of his poor relations, and the payment of the most trivial debts.

Having thus scrupulously attended to all the claims of affection, loyalty, and justice upon earth, he turned his thoughts to heaven, confessing himself, partaking of the Holy Sacrament, and complying with the other ceremonies of a devout Catholic. In his last moments he was attended by his son Diego and a few faithful followers. Surrounded by these devoted friends, he died on the 20th of May, 1506, being about fifty-five years of age. His last words were, "*In manus tuas, Domine, commendo spiritum meum.*" "Into thy hands, O Lord, I commend my spirit."

MAY

BIBLIOGRAPHY

CHRISTOPHER COLUMBUS. By Salvador de Madariaga. (London, Hollis and Carter, 1949.)

TO THE NEW WORLD, Being the Log of Christopher Columbus Voyage to America. Illustrated by John O'Hara Cosgrave ii. (London, Allen, 1944.)

THE DISCOVERERS. Translated from the French by Robert M. Coates, (London, 1929.)

CHRISTOPHER COLUMBUS. By Jacob Wasserman. (London, Secker, 1930.)

CHRISTOPHER COLUMBUS. By F. Chapman. (London, Bastien, 1944.)

THE TRUTH ABOUT COLUMBUS. By Charles Duff. (London, Grayson and Grayson, 1936.)

NARRATIVES OF THE DISCOVERY OF AMERICA. Edited by A. W. Lawrence. (London, Cape, 1931.)

SELECT LETTERS OF CHRISTOPHER COLUMBUS. Translated and edited by R. H. Major, F.S.A., 2 vols. (London, Hakluyt Society, 1930, vols. 65, 70.)

CHRISTOPHER COLUMBUS AND THE NEW WORLD OF HIS DISCOVERY. By Filson Young, 2 vols. (London, Grant Richards, 1906.)

CHRISTOPHER COLUMBUS, HIS LIFE, HIS WORK, HIS REMAINS. By John Boyd Thacher, 3 vols. (New York, Putnam, 1903.)

ADMIRAL OF THE OCEAN SEA. By Samuel Eliot Morison, 2 vols. (Boston, U.S.A., Little, Brown, 1942.)

THE LIFE OF CHRISTOPHER COLUMBUS. By Sir Clements Markham. (London, Murray, 1892.)

CHRISTOPHER COLUMBUS. By H. H. Houben. (London, Routledge, 1935.)

THE AGE OF DISCOVERY. Edited by A. P. Newton. (London, University of London Press, 1932.)

CHRISTOPHER COLUMBUS. Everyman's Library. (London, Dent.)

THE LIFE AND VOYAGES OF CHRISTOPHER COLUMBUS. By Washington Irving, 3 vols. Revised edition, (London, Murray, 1849.)

NOTE:—It is regretted that many of the above-mentioned list are today (October, 1949) out-of-print or temporarily unobtainable. It is possible, however, to obtain copies of these books from most Libraries.

GLOSSARY

OF

LATIN, FRENCH, SPANISH WORDS AND PHRASES FOUND IN THIS BOOK

Adios. Adieu, farewell.
Adelantado. Lieutenant-governor.
Alcalde. A justice of the peace.
Alcantara. One of the three ancient Spanish orders of Knighthood.
Alcayde. Governor of a castle or fort.
Alguazil. Similar to our police-constable.
Alpha and Omega. Names of the first and last letters of the Greek alphabet, often used to signify the beginning and end.
Anana. Pineapple.
Anjou. An ancient province of France.
Archipelago. A sea interspersed with many islands; the name generally applied to the Ægean Sea, situated between Europe and Asia, but in this volume refers to the islands in the Caribbean Sea.
Aristotle. A distinguished Grecian philosopher, born BC 384.
Ave Maria. A Roman Catholic prayer to the Virgin Mary. It literally means, *Hail Mary;* and is the commencement of the salutation which the angel addressed to the Virgin, when announcing to her that she should be the mother of Jesus.
Areytos. Sacred, heroic, and historic ballads of the natives of Hispaniola, or Haiti, or San Domingo, as the island is variously called.
Benedictine. An order of monks, founded by St. Benedict.
Bight. A bend or small bay between two points of land—a bay.
Bivouac. In this case, meaning to watch, or be on guard.
Bodega. A storeroom or wine-cellar.
Bottinas. Coverings for the legs.
Bustard. A common name of birds that often wade in the water for their food. They seldom fly, but use their wings to aid them in running. They congregate in flocks, and are usually found on open and level grounds.
Caballero. A knight, nobleman, cavalier.
Cabriolet. A light carraige, or one-horse chair.
Cacique. A native chief.
Calabash. A vessel made of a dried gourd-shell, or shell of the fruit of the calabash tree.
Calesa. A Spanish chaise with two wheels.
Caleséro. Driver of a calash.
Cape Bojador. On the western coast of Africa.

Cape Horn. Southern extremity of America.
Captain-general of the Navy. In Spain, the commander-in-chief of a fleet.
Caravel. A light, old-fashioned ship. Chiefly Spanish and Portuguese of the 15th-17th centuries.
Carthusian. A religious order of monks, founded by St. Bruno, in 1086.
Cassava. A bread made of the root of the yuca.
Castillanos. A Spanish coin.
Catalonians. Inhabitants of Catalonia.
Chaldaic. The language of the inhabitants of Chaldea, one of the most famous nations of Asia, Chaldea was the southerly part of Babylonia. It was formerly a fertile country, but is now barren.
Cibao. A district in the interior of Hispaniola, so named from its stony, sterile appearance.
Cipango. Japan.
Contrabandista. A smuggler.
Darien (Isthmus of). A narrow neck of land which connects North and South America.
Desperado. A desperate man.
Dominican. An order of monks founded by St. Dominic. He was born in 1170, and died at Bologna in 1221.
Don Quixote (Adventures of). Written by Cervantes, a distinguished Spanish writer, who was born in 1547, and died in 1616 at Madrid.
Ducat. A coin, varying in value.
Espanola. See Hispaniola.
Falconets. A light cannon.
Flamingo. A sea bird, usually red in colour.
Flores. One of the Azores Islands in the Atlantic Ocean.
Foray. Making a raid or hunting.
Franciscan. A religious order of monks, founded in 1209, by St. Francis of Assisi.
Furling. Rolling up and fastening the sails.
Giralda. A Spanish name for a vane or weathercock.
Gloria in excelsis Deo. "Glory to God in the highest", the commencing words of a Hymn of Praise.
Hacienda. Country house.
Hidalgo. A person of noble birth.
High Admiral. As used in this volume, admiral-in-chief.
High Altar. In Roman Catholic churches, there are several altars; the principal one is elevated above the others, and is called the high altar.
His Holiness. A title of the Pope.
Hispaniola, Haiti or San Domingo. One of the largest and most fertile of the West Indies Islands, named by Columbus Espanola, from a fancied resemblance to some of the beautiful provinces of Spain.
India, Indians. Names given to this country and to its inhabitants. Columbus, on his discovery of America, was under theimpression that it was the eastern coast of Asia. The name was retained with

the word "West" added, to distinguish the country from the East Indies. To-day the name West Indies is restricted to the islands lying between North and South America.

Junta. An administrative council,

Junto. A council.

Latine or Lateen. A triangular sail, frequently used by vessels in the Mediterranean Sea. This is usually fixed to the mast at an angle of 45°.

Martin Behem or Behaim. One of the most learned mathematicians and astronomers of his age, born at Nuremberg about 1430.

Mayorazgo. An entailed estate.

Muscatel or Muscadel. A sweet wine made from muscadines.

Ne plus ultra. Literally meaning: "nothing more beyond" "the uttermost part".

New World. America.

Nubian. Relating to Nubia, in the Anglo-Egyptian Sudan.

Nuncio. The Pope's ambassador.

Our Lady. A name by which the Virgin Mary is called by Roman Catholics.

Patents. Sign that one is entitled to something.

Pater Noster. The Lord's Prayer; so called from the first two Latin words signifying "Our Father".

Patios. Open spaces in front of, or behind houses.

Plato. A celebrated Greek philosopher, born about 429 B.C.

Posada. An inn.

Ptolemy. A celebrated geographer, mathematician, and astronomer.

Repartimientos. Partition, division, distribution.

Salve Regina. A vesper hymn to the Virgin Mary.

Santa. Saint.

See. The jurisdiction of a bishop.

Senor. Sir or master.

Siesta. The time for taking a rest after dinner, generally from one to three o'clock. In this volume it signifies the rest itself.

Terra Firma. Dry land.

Variation of the needle. Deviation of the magnetic needle of the compass from the true north point.

Vasco da Gama. A Portuguese, born 1460, died 1524, who discovered the sea-route to India.

Veering. Changing course.

Vega. Plain, or tract of land.

Venta. An inn.

Weather-boards. Boards placed to prevent the sea from breaking upon a vessel.

Yuca, Yucca, or Jucca. A name given to an American shrub, which grows to the height of three feet, and which has a white flower.

INDEX